To Jen

BLOOD AND BATTERY

Best wishes,

Lindsay.

BLOOD AND BATTERY

Murder, riot and theft in old Argyll

Lindsay Campbell

Copyright © 2021 Lindsay Campbell

The moral right of the author has been asserted.

Apart from any fair dealing for the purposes of research or private study, or criticism or review, as permitted under the Copyright, Designs and Patents Act 1988, this publication may only be reproduced, stored or transmitted, in any form or by any means, with the prior permission in writing of the publishers, or in the case of reprographic reproduction in accordance with the terms of licences issued by the Copyright Licensing Agency. Enquiries concerning reproduction outside those terms should be sent to the publishers.

Matador
9 Priory Business Park,
Wistow Road, Kibworth Beauchamp,
Leicestershire. LE8 0RX
Tel: (+44) 116 279 2299
Fax: (+44) 116 279 2277
Email: books@troubador.co.uk
Web: www.troubador.co.uk/matador
Twitter: @matadorbooks

ISBN 978 1800465 688

British Library Cataloguing in Publication Data.
A catalogue record for this book is available from the British Library.

Printed and bound in the UK by 4edge limited
Typeset in 11pt Adobe Garamond Pro by Troubador Publishing Ltd, Leicester, UK

Matador is an imprint of Troubador Publishing Ltd

Grateful thanks are due to the following people whose input to the research and writing of this work has been invaluable:

The staff and volunteers of Argyll & Bute County archives ("Live Argyll").
The staff and volunteers of The Argyll Papers.
The staff of the Historic Search Room, National Records of Scotland, Edinburgh.
The members of Inveraray Historical Society.
Dave and Fiona at Oban Computers.
The staff of Oban Library.
The volunteers of the Slate Islands Museum and Heritage Trust.

Laura Bennit; Mr.W.Cameron; Kay Liney; Ms D.Lumb; Mr.E.MacLellan; Mr.K.MacTaggart; Mark Mitchell; Elaine Stokes; Mrs D.Wyton.

Messers Jeremy Thompson and Joe Shillito, Ms Emily Dakin, and the staff at Troubador,

and especially SRN number 215263, who is always ready to proof-read!

ONE

The roads of Argyll have always been troublesome. Climate, wet peat or gravelly sub-soil around the heads of lochs, slipping hills and riversides, along with the difficulties of repairing the roads, when the state of them delays the very arrival of repair vehicles and materials, mean that life in the county is not easy at times. In former centuries, when it was only cattle or other stock, the odd pony and sledge and the tramp of human feet which flattened the turf into a road of sorts, such difficulties were easily overcome.

With the coming of the mid 1700s and the politics of post Jacobite Scotland, government armies (chasing rebels through the hills or seeking to impose some control on the population) soon discovered the difficulties of road travel in old Argyll. Sheer necessity meant that highways capable of conveying carriages, carts and modern armies were desperately needed. Good communication and map–making was also required by communities slowly modernising, with advances in engineering and industry creeping in from the cities. In the face of those advances, the turf roads through the hills, as useful as they were (and still are!) for rural dwellers, were hopeless when faced with changing times, and changing demands. The pace of life was quickening and the slowness of rural Argyll life needed to catch up with it – whether that rural Argyll life liked it or not![1]

Other changes were happening around the same time, changes that meant a certain Duke on the shores of a certain Argyll loch wasn't keen on living in a ramshackle 'pavilion' beside a derelict castle when he visited his town, nor on seeing sprawling poverty-stricken hovels and tenements infront of that castle. Needing a new castle, the Duke of Argyll was also determined to have a new town, and that on a new site, on the Rudha-na-h-Airde promontory.[2]

The Duke of the time was the brother of the man who'd seen the county through the war-torn years of the first Jacobite Rebellion.[3] This latter figure had died just before the second Rebellion,[4] leaving the duchy to Archibald, a trained lawyer, and acknowledged to be a shrewd industrialist, inelegant and bookish;[5] he arrived in the little fishing town on Loch Fyne, beside its almost derelict castle in summer 1744, already determined on creating a more harmonious landscape around his new home. [6]

Despite the difficulties with an intervening Jacobite Rebellion, transport, simple lack of furnishings, food and staff, a failing economy and a busy political scene, Duke Archibald somehow managed to make a start on his new castle and his new town.[7] As dour a man as he was, he seems to have made friends and to have some respect for all classes of people including those who were building his new properties,[8] and by 1759, although the old castle still stood, teetering over the brink of the river Aray, and edged by the old pavilions at its feet, the fine new castle was largely finished, with just some internal work, the dry-moat, and fittings to be completed.[9]

Down the road in the new town, or what was to become the new town, the situation was rather more haphazard. In what can only be described as a 25 acre building site,[10] only two private houses were standing, while a third was in the process of being erected.[11] What would later become elegant little gardens to the private houses, or the sites of fine new churches, villas and respectable tenements, were boggy fields, and tracks little better than linear mud-baths.[12]

The people occupying much of the headland were the workmen and their seniors, the drivers of carts carrying building materials from the pier, the masons bashing around with stone and tools, the smiths, wrights, lime-burners and gardeners, the labourers, the foremen and the long suffering architects battling the fickle demands of burgh committees, the Duke's 'admin boys' and the equally fickle Loch Fyne weather.[13]

On the northern half of this new town of Inveraray, the Duke had had a small bakehouse built,[14] and a great long garden wall, complete with an already mature beech avenue,[15] against which an inn had been built, still somewhat unfinished, and certainly not weatherproof. It stood facing the loch, with its grey three storey frontage, its ranks of windows and its central arch for carriages which came rattling poste haste from Glasgow along the newly laid road.[16] Finance had always been a big problem for Inveraray,[17] but soon after the inn had been built, the burgh council managed to scrape enough together, with donations from some worthy officials, to start work on the 'townhouse' or new tolbooth, just over the road from the inn.[18]

This new tolbooth and prison had a ceremonial laying of the foundation stones one spring day in 1755, with much pomp and circumstance and "joyful spectators", followed by dinner in the new inn next door.[19] From these hopeful beginnings, it all seemed to go downhill for the new tolbooth and it grew (a year late in completion), stone by local stone, and slate by Easdale slate, to be a matching edifice to the inn, not however being fully finished, inside or out, for many a long year, with a leaking roof and windows, inadequate foundations, initially no prison bars on the windows or doors, and the cells such ironwork was supposed to be part of "insufficient".[20] Outside, three doors were ranged along the front of the building, complete with railings and arched skylights above. One door opened directly onto the debtor's cell, which had a window and hearth. The matching door on the other side of the building's frontage opened onto a staircase, while the central door sealed off a 30ft long, 6ft wide corridor (euphemistically called 'The Piazza'), lit by two openings, barred like prison windows. It was here that, at regular intervals, the prisoners would be walked, backwards and forwards, to get some fresh air and exercise, but also to exhibit their plight to the passing public in the hope of such a display acting as a deterrent.[21] Infact this display of the miserable prisoners often fuelled the desire of Inveraray inhabitants to manufacture an escape for the petty thieves behind the bars, and it became quite a spectacle, and quite a common thing for someone to assist a prisoner escaping from Inveraray tolbooth.[22] What the display of prisoners on the 'piazza' of the tolbooth also did, at least most of the year, was expose them to the blast of the gales, sleat and rain coming off the loch, remind them what they were missing of everyday life outside the prison, and give them the opportunity to speak with friends who might be waiting outside to see them – whether for the good or bad.

The prison cells for all but the debtors comprised one at each end of the building, with no hearth, but a narrow window slit, while a central cell (presumably for the worst prisoners – murderers, traitors and repeat escapologists) was a little larger but with no lighting and equally no heating. A vaulted ceiling crossed the whole block, and the cells were later condemned as being damp, unsanitary and cold. Above the ground floor prison cells, the second storey of the tolbooth served as a court room, with presumably the jury room to one side. In the court room itself, there was a single hearth, windows looking out over the loch, and a staircase leading to the ground floor and up into the attic rooms, which quickly became a school.[23]

The punishments meted out to those incarcerated in the tolbooth, and later found guilty, were still as brutal as they'd been in former generations. The simple lack of an adequate tolbooth in the early years of the 1750s however did pose a problem on the occasion of one notorious trial, which the court was forced to conduct in the kirk.[24] A year later, with still no new tolbooth, two Argyll women were convicted, one of them the 80 year old Sarah Graham from Kintraw by Kilmartin, the other Anne Campbell, each of them hardened thieves, and old Sarah having stolen £900-worth of important paperwork from a Glasgow merchant's pocket at the Glassary market.[25] It was rare at this time to hang women at Inveraray (even the worst of petty female thieves were flogged, branded or banished[26]), so perhaps the harsh judicial atmosphere surrounding the previous year's trial still prevailed. Anne and Sarah were summarily hanged, probably at the 'spare' gallows site on what is now Newton, or as it was then known Gallowgate.[27]

As for the hardworking men who built the new tolbooth two years after Anne and Sarah were hanged, many were probably locals, doubtless living in their own homes in the old town, with some incomers amongst them, housed in the "hutts" built deliberately for them on the Gallowgate.[28] Clearly, these few small cottages couldn't house all the workmen, and amongst the local men at least one, an old soldier, lived in the 'pavilion' at the foot of the old castle.[29]

This veteran campaigner was John Campbell, and he was also one of the worthy group of men known even then as Chelsea pensioners. The retired soldiers who made up the now world-renowned institution had been receiving an official government pension since the late 1600s, not all of them living in Chelsea. In addition to those admitted into the Chelsea barracks, there was an 'out–pensioner' system, in which any veteran deemed suitable enough to apply for a military pension, was allowed to live where they wished whilst receiving such an allowance. Any prospective pensioners applying to Chelsea had to come with a recommendation from someone respectable, and for the old soldiers who normally lived at the other end of the country from Chelsea, it would have been a long and difficult process, as an applicant had to travel in person, with his referee, down south, the system eventually being altered so that the man could be interviewed in his home county.[30]

There were a few Chelsea out-pensioners in Argyll

in the old days (including Lachlan MacLachlan who lost his papers and got involved in an attempted pressing into the army in the 1760s[31]). The pensioner John Campbell who lived in Inveraray in 1759, may have been a former corporal or sergeant in the Argyll regiment, as he certainly seemed local and didn't later appear to be intimidated by a younger, stronger man, and was capable of expressing his opinions loudly without getting into a fight about it. Someone at Inveraray (perhaps even his senior commanding officer 'Colonel Jack', the Duke's cousin) had probably been his referee when he applied for his pension and he may have served at Culloden, after which the regiment was disbanded. To add to his Chelsea pension, John clearly did some labouring work for the Duke late in 1759.[32]

At this time, the main road into Inveraray, along the head of the loch and past the old Kilmalieu burial ground, had recently been built by the soldiers of the Argyll Fencibles regiment[33] – a body of volunteers, summoned from the populace, who although uniformed, armed, trained and waged like any other soldier, weren't obliged to leave the country, and often served as a form of Home Guard, especially if there was some sort of civil disobedience happening, or a military road that needed building. They'd been raised that same year of 1759 and followed hard on the heels of the old (then disbanded) Argyll regiment, even having Colonel Jack at their head.[34] The road they were building stretched from Dumbarton to the brink of the Duke's estate, where civilian labourers took over the task, leaving the Fencibles to their local policing duties. And to their alcohol.

Alcohol of course makes anyone more confidant and

uninhibited, and faced with some competition (civilian labourers building the avenue wall, the estate roads, bridges and offices, along with the new castle, against the recently arrived military engineers), it was natural that there'd be some tension among the labouring men of all types in Inveraray at the time. Tension in the town and on the new town building site was rife,[35] and one day in late December, in the streets of the old town, an argument started. The Chelsea pensioner John Campbell had just received a 20 shilling note as wages for a team of labourers amongst whom he worked (perhaps he was their foreman), and he went to get it changed at Andrew Fisher's house, presumably so he could share the money out. When he returned, he must have met a young private, Duncan MacFarlane from the Argyll Fencibles, as the two men started exchanging "high words" outside the Sheriff Clerk's house. This building had recently been replaced with a fine new house adjoining the new tolbooth over on the Rudha-na-h-Airde promontory[36], but clearly the Sheriff Clerk's old place was more familiar to the locals, and still used as a landmark. MacFarlane was with John Campbell's fellow labourers and perhaps he demanded some share in the 20 shilling wages, or perhaps at the end of a day's work, he was simply high on alcohol from one of the many wee changehouses in the old town.[37]

Whatever the cause of the argument, and at the exchange of those "high words", Duncan MacFarlane pushed John Campbell so violently that the older man finished up on the ground, gripping his belly in pain. He managed to right himself though, and, doubtless winded and in some shock, asked the bystanders to take MacFarlane away, and told the latter in no uncertain terms that he was uncivil. This only served to incite MacFarlane further, and he demanded whether Campbell had been addressing him. Yes, the old soldier said, (and one can see here the courage and fortitude of a man who'd clearly met a few contentious characters over the years, in or out of uniform!), he did mean that MacFarlane was uncivil, and he probably stood his ground against the younger man. At this, MacFarlane threatened to drive his fist through Campbell's belly and wash his hands in his blood; he began hitting the pensioner so hard that Campbell was stooping again in pain. The younger man didn't stop, raining further punches and kicks on the old veteran, presumably now on the floor again, and trying to defend himself against the strikes to breast, head and groin.[38]

As for the other men around at the time, several tried to intervene, but only one, Angus Sinclair, managed to pull MacFarlane away from John Campbell. Sinclair was a much respected member of the Duke's staff, from an equally respected Inveraray family (his brother's house was only just by where the fight was happening [39]), and it's not surprising that he would try to defend an old soldier, even though he came in for a beating himself as a result of it. MacFarlane picked up Sinclair bodily and threw him against a nearby lamp-post (the old town, like the new one later, was lit by oil street lamps at the hand of an appointed lamp-lighter), and threatened to put his fist through his body aswell. Eventually, the young soldier was dragged away from the scene, leaving Angus Sinclair injured, and John Campbell badly beaten, no doubt limping and bleeding heavily. Someone offered to take him for a dram, but he declined, saying he was "past it" and just wanted to walk home to his bed.[40]

Half an hour after old John Campbell had been battered and beaten by Private MacFarlane in the High street of Inveraray, some of the witnesses to the attack, the men who'd been in the street with him at the time, went to see how he was. They weren't heartened by what they saw. The man who'd not complained of sickness before, and who'd worked with them capably for several months now, was lying on his bed in the pavilions by the old castle, unable to swallow anything, "in a very bad way", and "greatly hurt" in the head and belly, and on the breast. Someone may well have sent for the doctor, probably John MacNab, who'd been serving the lower class people in the town for over twelve years, and had run a military hospital there before then.[41] Duncan MacFarlane's attack on John Campbell had probably broken the latter's sternum and a rib or two, aswell as possibly puncturing his liver, or other internal organs, with reverberation injuries to his head and slow internal bleeding that killed the old soldier within a few days.[42]

It wasn't very long before the attack was brought to the attention of the courts, and a warrant put out for the apprehension of Private MacFarlane, an application readily granted, and the young man taken to the tolbooth in the new town of Inveraray. There was already a thief there, Jean MacKay, and the authorities took no time in referring them both to the circuit court in Edinburgh, who were due to attend the town come spring.[43]

This relatively new system of justice had been instituted to replace the abolition of Heritable Jurisdiction a few years before. The Duke of Argyll, amongst other nobles who'd inherited the power of sitting in judgement in criminal courts, had had to give up his role of High Sheriff and Justiciar (in practise a Sheriff Depute or Justice Depute often sat in court in the Duke's place), and now the man who'd been his deputy in court took the role of Sheriff, with Edinburgh advocates taking the place of the old Justice Generals.[44] In order to hold a trial for a serious criminal case a visiting 'circuit court' comprising this Advocate, top lawyers, and a raft of court officials would turn up sporadically to deal with any cases which the Sheriff Court or Burgh Courts referred to them. Inveraray was on the West Circuit, and because of the nature of the terrain and roads (or lack of them!), the visits of the circuit courts weren't always speedy, pleasant occurrences.[45]

In the case of the trial of Duncan MacFarlane, accused of the murder of the old soldier John Campbell in Inveraray, some prior details were taken by Sheriff substitute John Richardson (his was one of the private houses already built on the new town site, but he certainly wasn't a trained lawyer, though he had a relative who was[46]), and the whole issue referred to the higher authorities in Edinburgh. That effectively, is where our knowledge of the case ends. It can be assumed that the usual procedure for the attendance of the circuit court happened, and Duncan MacFarlane faced the daunting prospect of being one of the first (if not the first) murder case tried in the new tolbooth. The visiting court officials would have been wined and dined at the new inn when they arrived, having travelled along the same military road which MacFarlane helped to build, and a formal procession made the following day, with town, burgh and court officials arranged in order, protected by soldiery and local constables, to reach the new tolbooth.[47] It being still winter, there were doubtless some comments as the windows and roof perhaps dripped on someone's shoulders or desk, and the various witnesses would be called up, and their testimonies translated from Gaelic. At the end of the proceedings, which may have taken more than a day, a jury (possibly only comprising Inveraray, or at least Loch Fyne men) made their declaration and the whole visiting court returned under equally formal procession to the inn, to depart the following morning for Edinburgh.[48]

Quite what the verdict of that jury was, we'll probably never know. With such a reliable witness as Angus Sinclair, surely no court could ignore MacFarlane's intentions when he started beating up John Campbell. There isn't however any record of a hanging at Inveraray at the time, and the regimental records for that early era, seem to have disappeared. If the charge of murder was found proven, MacFarlane may have been sentenced to transportation, or sent to an Edinburgh gaol until the harshest of sentences could be carried out. It wasn't uncommon for soldiers convicted of murder to be tried and hanged by a civilian court[49], and even if the murder charge was found Not Proven, and MacFarlane was only convicted of manslaughter ('culpable homicide' in the Scottish courts) or assault, any punishment (perhaps in an Edinburgh or Glasgow court, since he would still technically be a soldier) may have involved a flogging, and the heftiest of fines, which could make him a pauper if he was subsequently dismissed from the regiment.

All the records for this period of Argyll's history are scantier than for later or earlier decades, possibly due to the political situation, changes in the justice system and of course a flitting for the entire court from the old tolbooth to the new, with a gap of many months during which trials of any criminal must have been difficult, and holding onto court papers almost impossible. Much must have been lost or simply not bothered with in the huge administrative and governmental changes in the second half of the 1700s in Inveraray, and it was only with the onset of the final years of the century that the legal system in Argyll started churning out its accustomed vast amount of paperwork, to the delight of later historians, several of the carefully packaged sheets still marked ominously "Blood and Battery".[50]

Sadly the records for the Chelsea outpensioners at that same period aren't readily available either [51], and with such a common name in the county, old John Campbell may well be untraceable in what other Chelsea records remain, anyway. As a respected member of the labouring group at Inveraray, he was probably afforded a small military funeral at Inveraray's burial ground, back along the road nearer his old home, even if there doesn't appear to be a headstone to him. So must have passed many an old, respected, soldier at the time, but so it seems also passed the fiery private MacFarlane, leaving only his ill fame as the instigator of possibly the first murder tried in the new town of Inveraray, being certainly one of the builders of Duke Archibald's magnificent new military road, some of the walls and bridges of which still stand today, alongside the modern tarmac. The old roads of Argyll certainly could tell a tale or two of criminals, caught, convicted, hanged, escaped or acquitted, and the new roads soon to be built all over the county would bear an equal weight of criminal activities before long.

FOOTNOTES

1. The lack of good roads instigated the making of the map famous among historical researchers (Roy's map, available online on the National Library of Scotland Map Room website). The situation requiring better roads is exemplified by the trouble the new Duke of Argyll had when trying to access Inveraray after his succession. He eventually made it via Edinburgh and Glasgow, overland through Hell's Glen before crossing Loch Fyne from St.Catherine's (ref. "Inveraray and the Dukes of Argyll" by Ian G.Lindsay and Mary Cosh, published Edinburgh University Press,1973, pp.17-18,65-66, henceforth referred to as 'Inv&Dks').
2. "Records of Argyll" by Lord Archibald Campbell, published Blackwood and Sons, Edinburgh 1885, p. 49;Inv&Dks pp.12,15,25-26,27.
3. Inv&Dks p.3.
4. Ibid.
5. Ibid. pp.3,6-10.
6. Ibid. pp.10-12.
7. Ibid. pp.46-47,54ff.
8. Ibid. pp.3,68,100.
9. Ibid. pp.70,93,95,98,101.
10. Ibid. pp.266, with an acre being 120,583 sq.yds.
11. Ibid. and p.148.
12. Ibid. p.168-9.
13. Ibid. pp.56-57,73,79,84.
14. Ibid. p.266.
15. Ibid. p.121.
16. Ibid. pp.79-80,106,99,154-162.
17. Ibid. p.22.
18. "The Royal Burgh of Inveraray" by Alexander Fraser, published The Saint Andrew Press, 1973, p.48.
19. Inv&Dks pp.79-80.
20. Ibid. pp.162-4.
21. Ibid. pp.159,315-6.
22. "The Royal Burgh of Inveraray" by Alexander Fraser, published The Saint Andrew Press, 1973, p.48; "Odd incidents of Olden Times, or Ancient Records of Inveraray" by Peter MacIntyre, published Aird and Coghill, 1904, pp.77,33-4,316; "The Argyll Justiciary Records volume 2, 1705-1742" published by the Stair Society 1969, p.xvi-xvii; Inv&Dks p.316.

23. Inv&Dks pp.159,316;"The Royal Burgh of Inveraray" by Alexander Fraser, published The Saint Andrew Press, 1973, p.49.
24. "The Encyclopaedia of Scottish Executions, 1750-1963" by Alex F.Young, published Eric Dobby Publishing Ltd, Kent, 1998, pp.43-44; "The Royal Burgh of Inveraray" by Alexander Fraser, published The Saint Andrew Press 1973, p.35; Inv&Dks pp.77,78.
25. "The Encyclopaedia of Scottish Executions, 1750-1963" by Alex F.Young, published Eric Dobby Publishing Ltd, Kent, 1998,p.45.
26. Several criminal cases within "The Argyll Justiciary Records volume 2, 1705-1742" published by the Stair Society 1969, eg.pp.357,404,464. Between 1664 and 1742, it appears that the Inveraray courts (wherever they met) hanged only six women, as opposed to 52 men; see also the index of the above volume, which also covers references to volume 1.
27. Inv&Dks p.149.
28. Ibid. pp.148-9,174.
29. John Campbell can't have lived far from home at the time, since he wouldn't have been able, as badly injured as he was, to walk home in such a short timescale and we know the fight took place in the old town because of the reference to a lamp standard, such fixtures not yet being in place in the new town (see original trial notes SC54/10/5 in the National Records of Scotland, Edinburgh); The Royal Commission on the Ancient and Historical Monuments of Scotland, volume 7, Mid Argyll and Cowal, medieval and later monuments, published 1992, p.289.
30. theses.ncl.ac.uk/dspace; www.chelsea-pensioners.co.uk
31. Inveraray Burgh Court Processes, 1686-1825, deeds, bonds of caution etc 1710-1810, edited by Frank Bigwood, p.49 and 51.
32. National Records of Scotland, SC54/10/5; Inveraray Burgh Court Processes, 1686-1825, deeds, bonds of caution etc 1710-1810, edited by Frank Bigwood, p.49.
33. Inv&Dks pp.60,66,77,79-80,88,101,104,106,121-25,127,135-6; The Royal Commission on the Ancient and Historical Monuments of Scotland, volume 7, Mid Argyll and Cowal, medieval and later monuments, published 1992, p.114 and number 264.
34. The Argyll Fencibles commonly referred to in historic literature were the ones refounded c.1790, but there was an earlier regiment founded very soon after Culloden and on the back of the disbanding of the professional Argyll regiment, both of the latter being headed by Colonel Jack. Inveraray Burgh Court Processes, 1686-1825, deeds, bonds of caution etc 1710-1810, edited by Frank Bigwood, p.49; "A History of

Clan Campbell, volume 3, from the restoration to the present day", by Alastair Campbell of Airds, published Edinburgh University Press, 2004, pp.148,188,191,195-196,292; Inv&Dks pp. 60,66,77,88,101,104,121-25,127,135-6.
35. Inv&Dks p.67,80,90-92.
36. The Royal Commission on the Ancient and Historical Monuments of Scotland, volume 7, Mid Argyll and Cowal, medieval and later monuments, published 1992, pp.433-4 .
37. National Records of Scotland, SC54/10/5.
38. Ibid.
39. Angus Sinclair conveyed the new Duke's valuables to Rosneath in 1749, not something which would have been asked of anyone untrustworthy; he was later witness to a baptism of one of his new servants (Argyll Papers archives ref.ARG/06/A/02/01,1749 rentals; Inv&Dks p.89;"The Royal Burgh of Inveraray" by Alexander Fraser, published The Saint Andrew Press, 1973, p.173).
40. National Records of Scotland, SC54/10/5.
41. Argyll Papers archives, ref.bundle 3643,1747; "The Campbells of the Ark, men of Argyll" volume 2, by Ronald Black, published John Donald, 2017, pp.351,467,567.
42. Testimony of B.Mower SRN HVC NCDN CMB.
43. "Odd incidents of Olden Times, or Ancient Records of Inveraray" by Peter MacIntyre, published Aird and Coghill, 1904, p.26.
44. Inv&Dks, pp.151-3,66; "The Argyll Justiciary Records, volume 1, 1664-1705" published by the Stair Society, 1949 p.xiii.
45. See footnote 47 (below) and the occasion (see chapter 6) when a visiting judge complained because he hadn't been greeted at Dalmally by a carriage to convey him to town.
46. "The Campbells of the Ark, men of Argyll", volume 2, by Ronald Black, published John Donald, 2017, p.126.
47. Although there isn't any description of the visit of a circuit court at this time, one can perhaps get an idea of the process from the visit of the court in 1908, allowing for the fact that there may have been less people in the procession in the 1700s (eg.no police officers), and perhaps not as many uniformed staff ("The Royal Burgh of Inveraray" by Alexander Fraser, published The Saint Andrew Press, 1973, pp.65-67).
48. Ibid.
49. Several cases in "The Encyclopaedia of Scottish Executions, 1750-1963", by Alex F.Young, published Eric Dobby Publishing Ltd, Kent, 1998, eg. pp.74,67, 63-4,62-3,57.
50. Remaining records of the sheriff court exist from 1748

(SC54/10/4), but are rather restricted re.sentences and some supporting evidence until c.1795, while the circuit court records, clearly lodged at Inveraray from a similar date, appear to have been lost or relocated for much before then. The "blood and battery" references are on documents within the SC54/10/8 collection.
51. www.chelsea-pensioners.co.uk

TWO

In the 1970s, as part of the great reshuffle of administrative districts and counties in Scotland, an area on the very northern fringes of Argyll was disjoined from the county after being part of the district for centuries.[1] The parish of Ardnamurchan, and the area around the village of Acharacle was included in this administrative reshuffle, turning over to Inverness-shire an area which had seen some crucial historic action in the 18th century, in the wake of the Second Jacobite Rebellion.[2] Amongst the people living in Ardnamurchan at the time was one Duncan MacLean, a tacksman in Sunart, with (presumably) his wife and young family. Duncan's farm was at Derryghairve,[3] just up the hill from Acharacle, a spot now swallowed up by the forestry plantation, possibly even ploughed into oblivion, but still remembered locally. Unfortunately, the district of Acharacle was also known for another, rather more sinister, quality; one local adage, spoken within living memory, says that if you're looking to be murdered, go to Acharacle. Certainly there would appear to have been more than one killing (or at least tragic accident) occuring in Acharacle parish, with the peninsula's autonomy, and the numerous coastal inlets (effectively small-time ports) contributing in former times to the sort of serious crime only happening in the towns.[4]

In earlier times however, and just after the Jacobite Rebellion, when the Redcoats were chasing Ardnamurchan rebels around the peninsula, Duncan MacLean in Derryghairve had three young sons: John the eldest, Hugh the middle one who had a learning disability, possibly a congenital disorder characterised by difficulties in hearing, speech and comprehension. Then there was young Allan. Hugh, despite his disability, could at least pay attention to his lessons, read somewhat, and fulfill what life and society expected of him. Young Allan MacLean had the same learning disability as his brother, but his disorder was far worse. He was known locally as 'Dumbie', (because of his speech difficulties, not because of his intellectual problems) and it was a name applied, it seems, affectionately by his neighbours, despite our modern disinclination to the use of such terms. The boys' father said he was far too busy caring for his middle son to pay any attention however, to Allan; so Allan effectively went feral.[5]

Over the fields, hills and woods of Ardnamurchan, young Allan MacLean roamed to his heart's content, getting fed at anyone's door, doing the occasional odd job for a neighbour (and performing it very satisfactorily it turns out), aswell as picking up any appealing object he came across and keeping it as his own. When challenged with the location of such objects (a pair of boots, a gun or a plaid is quoted) he would readily show searchers where he'd left them – on one occasion 12 miles away, and never close to his own home. With no social awareness, he would climb trees, squeal, and wander the golden sands of his home parish and beyond, in fair weather or foul, night or day. As fondly as he was held by the locals, by the time Allan reached his teens, he was becoming challenging to care for, if his father cared for him at all, and there isn't any mention in the old records of the boys' mother. Allan's habit of confiscating any goods left in the open was becoming rather difficult, and on one occasion, a passing pedlar bribed him with a whistle so that he would reveal the location of the 'stolen' goods.[6] A very wise move indeed, probably enabling anyone, hearing the playful blowing of the whistle, to hide their boots and plaid before Allan came along. One assumes that Allan found the whistle entertaining because of the vibrations, or just the fact that it was a small, silvery object which drew people's attention to him, since his deafness would have made him oblivious to the sound.

There was a darker side to this situation however than a wise pedlar with a whistle and a fondly regarded boy with a congenital disorder. Allan's father clearly cared little for his youngest son. He later told the authorities that he'd heard many complaints about the boy, and that despite his efforts to restrain and discipline him, he escaped and continued his 'thieving' ways. He had no sense of religion or a deity, and infact went out at night looking at the moon. His brother Hugh had made signs to him that he would be punished if he didn't attend to his religious exercises, but it was all to no effect. Allan continued being "remarkably defective in point of judgement and understanding". So the beatings started. Duncan MacLean would beat his youngest son relentlessly in order to force him to change his ways, and sadly, there was an effect of sorts from these beatings, although perhaps not the effect Duncan had wished for.[7]

Down at Acharacle, another farmer (one gets the impression he was rather better off than the MacLeans), Ewan Cameron in Acharacle had cause to do some engineering work on his tenancy. What he needed was a sturdy auger[8], perhaps to drill down into the sub-soil to make a well, and it turned out that Duncan MacLean up at Derryghairve had one which would fit the bill. It seems that men and their love of tools hasn't changed, as someone went up the hill to ask if Ewan could borrow the device. When the day came for passing over the auger, Mrs.Cameron and her teenage son Duncan, came to Derryghairve. There would doubtless have been some polite conversation, some promises to give the auger back as soon as it had served its purpose, and young Duncan Cameron headed down the hill on his own for home. Perhaps Mrs.Cameron stayed a little longer, or went onto another neighbour afterwards. It would be the last time she saw her son alive.

It can't have been long after Mrs.Cameron returned home that she and her husband realised that their son was missing – along with the auger. The first port of call would of course have been the MacLeans at Derryghairve, and off Duncan MacLean and Ewan Cameron went into the woods and moors surrounding the farm, looking for the teenager. Eventually, they came across a daunting sight. A rough track had been made leading from the moor into the woods, and along this track something bloody had been dragged, disturbing the twigs and leaves and mud. But still there was no sign of Duncan Cameron, let alone the auger the MacLeans had loaned to his father.

For some reason untold in the old records, at this stage Duncan MacLean decided they should return to

Derryghairve to see if Allan knew of the other boy's location. There's a hint that Allan had had some mud and rain on his clothes that day, but considering his habits, that could hardly have been an important factor in the case. He did seem to know something though, as when his father and Ewan Cameron tried to persuade him to come with them to the moor, he "struggled hard against the going". In the end, both the persuasion of his father, promising him a party afterwards if he showed them where Duncan Cameron's body was, and the threatenings of his eldest brother with a leather strap, convinced Allan to go along with them to the moor. After further searching, and on Allan's prompting, the "greatly mangled" remains of an almost naked Duncan Cameron was found, hidden by leaves and branches in a burn, with his face, head and temples deeply wounded "as if made by a stone". The ground around was bloody, and the boy's clothes, shoes and the loaned auger were all missing.

Clearly still present at the murder site, young Allan MacLean was promptly tied up with rope (which rather begs the question, why did the men have rope with them?), and someone took him back to Derryghairve, leaving the initial two searchers to continue the hunt for the deceased boy's clothes and the auger. Again, having no luck in their search, they returned to the farm, where before they even entered the farmhouse, someone brought Allan out and forced him to point out where the clothes and auger were hidden. Into an adjoining barn, the dead boy's father and Duncan MacLean went, still having no luck in the search until Duncan happened to look upwards, and there, hidden in the rafters, was a creel, stuffed full of something. When brought down, it revealed its contents as a "good deal" of old scraps of timber, and at the bottom, the shoes and clothes and auger – strangely, all of them clean.[9]

That seems to have sealed the deal for Duncan MacLean. He soon had his youngest son bundled up with ropes again, and set out for Inveraray. The journey would have been a long one – probably partly by sea, from Salen or Kilchoan through the Sound of Mull, landing at Oban, then not much more than a hamlet, with a couple of inns, and a few fishermen's cottages,[10] and down to Inveraray, perhaps via the old drove road to Kilchrenan, and onto the military road at the other side of the loch and which had been so recently finished[11] After several days on the road (during which one presumes MacLean was happy to leave his farm and the care of Hugh in his eldest son's hands), they turned up on Sheriff Campbell's doorstep in the newly built town of Inveraray. Well, not quite newly built. There was still a lot of work to do, but at least there was somewhat of an improvement on the state of the place when the old soldier had died at the hands of a younger colleague a few years before. The Sheriff's house was a new one, small and perfectly adequate, but not quite finished internally, and sitting next door to the fine big tolbooth on what is now Front street.[12] It's dubious as to whether Sheriff Campbell would have lodged in this house at the time, or in the old one attached to the semi-ruined castle. If he was at the new house though, the doorstep currently there may be the same on which Duncan MacLean stood with young Allan that day in 1761, and knocked, hoping to leave the boy in the care of the court. But the Sheriff wasn't in, and his servants, on the situation being explained to them, didn't want to take Allan in, incase he did one of his notorious escape acts. Duncan MacLean didn't want to take him back home, incase he killed again – all the neighbours, he said, would turn against the family, and he wanted Allan "disposed of" as the court thought fit. Those very words strike compassion into modern hearts, and it seems struck a similar feeling into the hearts of the people back in Acharacle. One lady later wrote to the court saying how Allan had delivered cloth for her in Strontian, taking the parcels to her customers, whilst even the dead boy's family didn't speak against the MacLeans. It seems it was only Allan's family who had anything against him, but still there was talk of a trial, and gaol and the boy had to be kept somewhere in the town. At first (perhaps the gaol was full, or deemed too distressing or insecure for him) Allan was given lodging in the garrison, ie.part of the old castle, before being transferred to the gaol below the courthouse in the great grey tolbooth building.[13] And that, like the case of soldier MacFarlane just two years before, is the last we hear of young Allan MacLean. The one thing that we can be sure of, is that he wasn't hanged. There is evidence that there was only one hanging in Inveraray between the demolition of the old town and the end of the century, and that had been a few years previous when the two women thieves were convicted.[14] The state of Allan's mind was also likely to have not been suited to him standing trial. Later in the century, rules were laid down as to how a court should proceed when someone who was apparently ill was accused of a serious crime, but at the time of Allan's arrival at Inveraray, a decision about whether someone was fit to stand trial (and understood what he/she was accused of) was left to the individual courts and their prosecutors.[15]

The likeliest scenario is that Allan was lodged in a secure place, possibly still the gaol for a while, until someone could organise a care system for him. It was common at the time to treat such disorders by blood letting and purging to calm the patient, followed by aggressive treatments such as solitary confinement or restraints if the person was themselves aggressive, or by lodging them in a caring household, such as that of a local doctor or kirk minister, if the patient was able to fill their days relatively profitably or calmly, as it seems Allan had the capability of in the right circumstances.[16] There isn't any evidence of a headstone in Kilmalieu burial ground for him, and the kirk minutes which sometimes recorded a payment for a funeral, don't seem to fulfill that purpose at the time in Inveraray.[17] He may have died relatively young and we can only hope that there were sincerer hearts and kinder heads in Inveraray than in Allan's own family.

All we're left with, as with so many cases in the records of the time, is a series of questions and a number of features which stand out to modern minds.

Despite what Allan's father later claimed in court, the boy was clearly able to conceive of the consequences of his own actions, otherwise why did his eldest brother threaten him with a leather strap or his father promise him a party if he showed them where Duncan Cameron's body was? Could it be that he had the ability to conceive the consequences of his actions if he was told about them there and then, and/or had experienced such a situation before, but couldn't do so on his own; he didn't possess the initiative. If this was the case (and the testimony of the neighbour who later said he did some parcel carrying for her would appear to support the theory), it may mean that he'd experienced something on the moor which scared him, hence why he "struggled against" the going back there.

In addition, if Allan had ever hit anyone with a rock, accidentally or deliberately, his father would have been only too glad to say so in court – he told the court about anything else anti-social that his son did (looking at the moon, squealing, climbing trees etc). So if Allan had hit young Duncan Cameron with a rock, where did he get the concept of it from, since he clearly didn't have the initiative to conceive of such actions in the first place? And it seems strange that Duncan's clothes and shoes were clean, the boy, or his body, obviously having been stripped before he was dragged into the woods.

There's no doubt that if Allan had seen Duncan with the auger, he may have wanted it and thought that he had the right to take it. So where did the rock come into it? Did Duncan take his shoes and breeches off to paddle in the burn on the way home, then fight Allan for the auger, fall in the burn, and receive the wounds to his face and head that way? The claim that Duncan's body was "greatly mangled" doesn't align however with a simple fall into a burn. Even if he'd climbed a tree in pursuit of Allan and the auger, modern studies show that any head injuries he'd sustained from a fall wouldn't have added up to a "greatly mangled" face and head.[18] The mangling does appear to have come about due to the body being dragged into the woods from the moor. Even if someone had hit Duncan with the auger, greatly mangling his face, it would appear to have been thoroughly cleaned afterwards, which isn't something one could imagine Allan doing, him not having the initiative to conceive of why the auger should be cleaned.

All we can be certain of is that Duncan Cameron had died by a traumatic injury from a rock on the moor near Derryghairve, and that Allan MacLean had been close by when this had happened, the dead boy's clothes and shoes then being removed, before his body was dragged into the woods and hidden. The clothes, shoes and the loaned auger were subsequently stashed back home in the byre (in itself uncharacteristic, since Allan had always hidden his findings away from home before then). Whoever's hand had been on the death-inflicting rock, Allan had clearly been distressed enough by the occasion to not want to return to the spot. It all comes back to the murder weapon: who wielded the rock? With his clear inability at using initiative, Allan MacLean doesn't seem to have been the one. It appears that someone else had been on the moor that day, possibly with Allan, or possibly discovering both boys soon afterwards, Duncan perhaps unconscious after a fall in the burn, and a fight with Allan. Did the latter's father or eldest brother, hoping to have Allan convicted and out of their hands at last, administer the coup de grace to young Duncan Cameron, then drag him into the woods to hide him? Certainly, from Allan's prior behaviour, he hadn't shown reluctance to lead searchers to his stash of found goods before, so why would he be reluctant this time?

The very least which one can say about the tragedy, is that, in the words of Ewan Cameron himself, the death of his son was an "unfortunate accident". Today, in the forestry plantation by Acharacle, the birds sing, the martens scatter, the wild flowers sprawl over the rocks in the clearings, but nothing is left on the ground of the once-thriving farmstead of Derryghairve. The only remnants of that time which are left, are local memory and the tragic story in the court records of two boys, one gradually going feral and getting more wise attention from a passing pedlar than his own family, the other's life cut short, whilst in the background is a shadowy figure who may have had more of a hand in the tragedy than he cared to admit.

FOOTNOTES

1. An administrative plan held by Argyll & Bute County archives ("Live Argyll"), Manse Brae, Lochgilphead showing the new boundary lines of the county c.1975.
2. Several sources, especially those describing the flight of Cameron of Lochiel after Culloden, eg. "The Campbells of the Ark, men of Argyll in 1745" volume 1, by Ronald Black, published John Donald, 2017, p.276-7, 413-5, 558-9; "The Campbells of the Ark, men of Argyll in 1745" volume 2, by Ronald Black, published John Donald, 2017, pp.83,88,391 etc.
3. SC54/10/6, available in the National Records of Scotland historic search room.
4. Testimony of Mr.W. Cameron, Glasgow, formerly of Acharacle, to whom the author is indebted.
5. SC54/10/6, available in the National Records of Scotland, Edinburgh.
6. Ibid.
7. Ibid.
8. Described in the old records as a whimble: "Scots Theasaurus" edited by Iseabail MacLeod and others, published Polygon, Edinburgh, 1999, p.317.
9. SC54/10/6, available in the National Records of Scotland historic search room.
10. Royal Commission on the Ancient and Historic Monuments of Scotland, Argyll, volume 2 (Lorn), 1974, pp.242-243.
11. Ibid. pp.295-6; General Roy's Map, available online via the National Library of Scotland Map Room website (maps.nls.uk).
12. The Royal Commission on the Ancient and Historical Monuments of Scotland, volume 7, Mid Argyll andCowal, medieval and later monuments, published 1992 volume 7, pp.433-4; Inv&Dks p.171.

13. SC54/10/6, available in the National Records of Scotland historic search room.
14. "The Encyclopaedia of Scottish Executions, 1750-1963" by Alex F.Young, published Eric Dobby Publishing Ltd, Kent,1998, p.45.
16. rcpe.ac.uk; "Therapies for Mental Ailments in 18th century Scotland" a paper by R.A.Houston, 1998, published by St.Andrew's University, available online; historyforensicpsych.umwblogs.org
17. CH2/190/3 in National Records of Scotland, Edinburgh.
18. A general conclusion from several studies made of head injury trauma as a result of falls indicates that, if young Duncan Cameron fell from a tree of about 15ft high or more, and did hit his head on landing, the injuries would be more likely to occur at the back or top of his head, rather than his face, and that he would probably survive such trauma. See www.sciencedirect.com/science/article/pii/soo20138370801206

THREE

"Campbeltown loch, I wish ye were whisky" goes the old song. Among the towns and villages in old Argyll, Campbeltown wasn't unusual in Victorian times in having a fair few distilleries among its streets; fine upstanding institutions with well-respected managers and staff.[1] A century earlier, it's acknowledged that there was only one legal distillery (this at the time of Robert Burns' visit[2]), but it's doubtful even if this existed in the 1750s. What was known to exist in and about Campbeltown then however, were the excisemen, invariably local men with crucial experience in uniform and at sea, and ideally willing to both take orders and use their initiative, when faced with weapon-wielding smugglers and illegal distillers. Their job it was to see that anything taxable (in Campbeltown's case, usually alcohol) was declared, and the correct fees paid to the correct person in the correct custom house.[3]

At this date, the goods being imported into Argyll, and having to have taxes paid on them included everything from soap, silk, coal and French wine to hair oil, salt, tobacco, and Norwegian timber. With things such as Irish herrings or leather also being imported[4], it's natural that the local producers often felt rather put out, but at least if the importers paid their taxes, the local producers would be at an economic advantage. Unfortunately, such local producers also included the distillers of whisky, which when produced for the consumption of one's own family and immediate friends (especially if one wasn't charging people for the privilege) was technically legal. When it came to the produce of the little illegal whisky stills scattered about the hills and wooded islands of Argyll, so much of it was sold, untaxed, to the smaller public houses that the infamous excisemen had a difficult task.

Unless those excisemen were somewhat – shall we say? – 'friendly' with the distillers and smugglers. Almost as notorious in legend as the corrupt nobleman sitting in judgement on a smuggler[5], is the exciseman who lets rather too many smugglers slip under the net. In 18th century Campbeltown, there was at least one of these corrupt excisemen, and he wasn't the lovable rogue which legend so often likes to portray such men as being.

Daniel or Donald MacLarty may have come from a long-standing Kintyre family, with close connections to the sea, and the red-tape of commerce in and around Campbeltown. Like any close-knit community, there appears to have been a degree of nepotism in the town at the time, like in Inveraray, with 'jobs for the boys' usually available for those with a particular surname. There'd been MacLartys in the Campbeltown area for decades, with some very respectable trades,[6] but Danny MacLarty who rented a croft at Askomil in 1754, with his mother and married sister and her husband living close by, wasn't such a respectable member of his family. He'd been involved in fights and riots locally and may even have been present at a murder in later years, while the old records state that he was familiar to the authorities, and not from his supposedly official status of exciseman.[7] His croft of Askomil, on the outskirts of Campbeltown, was at the time a rural holding, surrounded by enclosed fields and overlooking the steel grey waters of the bay, an hours walk from the town limits.[8] The road ran behind the farm-house, (not as now in front of it[9]) and was situated on rising land, with a burn which emerged or sank into the ground variously, culminating downhill in a spring just out of sight of the farm buildings.

One day in September 1754, Danny MacLarty was at home at Askomil, when he heard shouting outside. His sister Jean was calling to him, telling him that she'd arrived back home, after her solo trip into town where she'd been partaking of the notorious Campbeltown alcohol (it isn't stated whether it was whisky, legal or illegal she'd been imbibing). Danny knew that his brother-in-law was away from home at the time, probably out with the boat, fishing or carrying freight to and from Glasgow, and he was clearly a man who believed firmly in a married woman being a chattel of her husband, as he stormed outside (his own statement says that she'd forced his door, but there's some doubt about that), intent on haranguing Jean for going into town without John beside her.[10]

When he arrived at the Stirling's house, he found his sister was inside, but still of course as drunk, and still as shouty. She gave back as good as she got in the argument, hitting him with an iron brander and pulling his hair, although she missed a second attempt to hit him, as he grabbed her hands and forced her to the ground. "Several strokes" were "given and received" between the two of them, and so serious was the altercation that old Mrs.MacLarty called on a neighbour to intervene.[11]

John MacAlester also lived at Askomil, and his attention may have been alerted already, as he was at his byre door by the time he heard Mrs. MacLarty calling on him to go to the Stirling's house "and help save lives". When he ran over to the house and burst in, Danny had forced his sister onto her own bed, and was attempting to keep hold of her. When he saw MacAlester, Danny dragged Jean up off the bed and tried to pull her out of the door, Jean still fighting gamely, even pulling MacAlester's hair in mistake for her brother's.

At this point, Danny returned to his own house, probably not wanting anyone to witness his further ill-treatment of his sister, and the neighbour also returned to his work in the byre.[12]

Jean however, was still somewhat capable of creating further rumpus, and she followed her brother, shouting and getting back into his house again. According to Danny's later statement, she also broke a large spinning wheel, although quite how she managed that he doesn't say. Such devices are known to get damaged, commonly on the rim or the legs, but to do so deliberately, aware that it brought in a vital income for her own mother and sister, is hard to believe.[13] It seems therefore that Danny had either exaggerated this part of the incident, lied outright, or it was a flashpoint in his assault on Jean. As for the latter, having perhaps been thrown out of the house, she left but was back again twenty minutes later, demanding some tobacco pipes (it's not clear in the court records whether she'd previously loaned them to Danny or wanted to borrow them). He threw some out of the window at her, but as the old clay pipes readily did, they shattered on the ground outside. Further angered at this, Jean threw a stone at Danny's window in return, breaking it and fuelling her brother's anger in the process.

The argument returned to the Stirling's house, with Danny following Jean back there, where she threw more stones out of the window at him, to no avail, as he climbed in through another window, grabbed her, tied her up and slung her on the bed. At some stage around now, the argument started to become disturbing. Mrs MacLarty had already called on John MacAlester for help again, but (perhaps used to these fights, and intimidated by Danny MacLarty's temper) he refused to come and help a second time. Some time around then however, both he and another witness saw Jean, wrists tied and with a rope round her neck, walking, badly beaten, downhill towards the well and out of sight of anyone at the farm. Infact the only people who could have seen what was about to happen at the well, would have been either on the loch or the shore, far below, and effectively blind to the details of any potential assault there. Following Jean to the well was another MacLarty sister and Danny, whilst old Mrs. MacLarty returned in panic to the farm saying that they'd been strangling Jean at the well with a hemp rope. Whatever had been intended down in the fields, out of sight of Askomil farm, Jean Stirling eventually emerged to the view of her neighbours, alive but very badly beaten, and still tied up. Now though, she wasn't fighting back any more. Danny and the other sister were still with her, and when, near the farm houses, they let go of her, her brother kicked her until she fell down. The next anyone saw of Jean was when she was back in bed, where Danny had thrown her, still with the rope round her neck and her hands tied. One witness who saw her the following evening, declared that he thought she was dying, and it took the attention of one of the Campbeltown surgeons to bring her speech back.[14]

Two days later (perhaps when John Stirling returned home from the boat), Danny MacLarty was called up to account for his behaviour to a committee including the surgeon, a lawyer and a few other local notables. He confessed to the beating, and was cautioned and kept in the Campbeltown tolbooth until he could find someone to stand surety for his future conduct, along with enough money to pay a 200 mark fine (around £40 sterling[15]). With such a hefty sum imposed on Danny MacLarty, the Campbeltown sheriff clearly thought him worthy of a severe punishment, so quite why he was still in the job of exciseman two years later, is a mystery.

Despite Danny's 'great' spinning wheel being allegedly broken by his sister in the argument that fateful September, it was clearly in good enough order to enable him to do business with one Richard Robison, weaver in Campbeltown. It was a common practise at the time for someone to spin their own fleeces, then take the results to a local weaver to be made into cloth.[16] Danny MacLarty being who he was though, the business between him and the local weaver was never going to be jovial, and by the end of summer, he was appealing to the Sheriff Court to have a lawburrows (injunction) taken out on Robison, whom he claimed had "an evil will and malice" towards him. MacLarty had no idea why the weaver felt that way, but he also claimed he'd induced a whole load of other people to trouble and molest him, threatening "harm and slaughter" to him, and demanding that Robison be apprehended, fined or cautioned.[17] This is classic litigious behaviour of Danny MacLarty, and he may infact be the same person who's recorded in later years as leading the application of a group of sailors who took their employer to court for failing to pay their wages, or on another occasion was summoned to the same court, along with many others, for contravention of the excise act.

It wasn't however until eight years after Danny MacLarty's attack on his sister Jean that his name turns up in the Campbeltown court records in any great capacity. He'd evidently been occupied in his excise job for some years now, and going by the behaviour of some of the locals, was held in a certain degree of nervous, begrudged respect. Up until this point no-one apart from his own sister and the local weaver had had the guts to challenge Danny out of court. He was about to get a taste of his own medicine however, and from someone younger, smaller and with less social 'clout' than him. An angry teenager.

One day in February 1761, Danny had had cause to go over to Gigha as part of his job, 'surveying' what was there which needed taxing; obviously not a very popular venture, and the passengers on the return journey may not have been very comfortable with the exciseman on board. They included a local merchant, a tenant farmer from Clachan and a soldier from the Argylls, who in the absence of a proper quay at Tighanloan had clearly volunteered to give anyone who required it a piggy-back ride through the water to the shore. Just before they left Gigha, an apprentice sailor from Campbeltown had come down to the ferry, asking for passage, although he didn't have the money to pay the fee. No-one seemed to mind, and the lad hopped on board.[18]

According to all the witnesses, the journey over to

Tighanloan was unremarkable. Danny however later told the court the boy had been swearing at the other passengers, and they'd threatened him in return, inducing Danny to act as his protector, an unlikely role for him, especially since he was supposed to be piloting the ferry into Tighanloan at the time. Once they pulled up at the mainland shore, and while the ferryman was seeing to his vessel, the soldier began piggy-backing the other passengers onto dry land. When it was the teenager's turn, he had great fun, splashing the soldier as they went, by slapping a stick against the water, much to the annoyance of both soldier and Danny MacLarty, who was in the close vicinity. When the men protested, the teenager, in classic fashion, only splashed about even more, declaring that he would wet the soldier to the skin, and threatening Danny similarly.[19]

Not a one for ignoring a threat, MacLarty took this as an invitation to start an argument, and the boy was happy to oblige, landing out at the older man with the same stick he'd been splashing everyone with earlier, and daring anyone to take it off him. He was in the burn by then, a burbly seepage of water coming through the salt marsh, and bending round onto the parchment coloured sands, the lack of a proper pier meaning that the boat would pull up wherever it could just south of the current pier. The shoreline has since receded (apparently taking the road with it and forcing a new road to be built further inland[20]), but the coast would still be as open to the wind on a February day as it is now, and in the teeth of such a sea wind, there's no wonder the passengers didn't like being splashed with water by the teenage tearaway who'd come over with them from Gigha. It was therefore with some harsh words exchanged between Danny MacLarty and the teenager, that Danny managed to grab the boy's staff and wrestle it from him, while hitting, threatening him, and getting thoroughly drenched in the process. He later told the court that the boy had even tried to hit him with a rock from the burn, which may have been the case, although no witnesses could testify to it.[21]

Clearly however Campbeltown teenagers aren't prepared to be beaten by a bully bigger than themselves, and as soon as he could, the lad wriggled away, ran to another passenger, grabbed the man's own staff and took a swing at Danny MacLarty's head. The strike hit home, but when he attempted a second one, the exciseman (in a move ironically similar to his actions in his sister's house years earlier) managed to prevent the strike by grabbing hold of the staff, and hitting back at the teenager. Not only hitting back, but repeatedly striking and beating the lad, so he finished up on his back in the burn, bloodied and bruised about the mouth, neck, head and "other parts", with broken teeth, swollen cheeks, and fearing for his life. Some of that may have been melodrama, coupled with the classic exaggeration any prosecution was wont to put into the criminal charges, but the lad certainly seems to have been very badly injured, whether Danny left him for dead or not. The latter certainly went off as soon as his victim was "got rid of", while the ferryman, and others, eventually realising what was happening, and maybe intimidated by MacLarty's presence, came over to the burn to help the teenager.[22]

At the time, there appears to have been a building in the crook of the burn (gone by the 19th century, along with the receding coastline[23]), and this may have been the Tighanloan inn at the time, perhaps transferred to its current site when the road was rebuilt further away from the shore. Certainly the present location of the inn would seem to be a rather long way to take such a badly injured boy, but wherever the building was, the young lad was taken there. A surgeon came to see him, and he was given "all possible care", even though Danny MacLarty himself later showed up, and there were further harsh words exchanged between the two of them.[24]

Nevertheless, the teenager's injuries were bad enough for someone (presumably his father, or his employer) to take the case to court, and within three weeks Danny MacLarty, the exciseman who'd been in Campbeltown tolbooth for his brutal attack on his sister seven years previously, was there again. This time the charge was more serious: he was accused of "barbarous, cruel and inhumane practises" against the Campbeltown teenager, and there was solid evidence of it, in the form of the surgeon's report.[25]

MacLarty's own statement in court comes over as laughable, in the way he claimed to have acted so irreproachably and mildly: he would "allow no man" to hurt the lad while on the journey over, since the other passengers had threatened him; he advised the boy to run away from the (supposedly) angry soldier while Danny had "desired him peaceably" to stop splashing everyone, "never lifting a hand or foot" to the boy. He didn't even believe that the boy's injuries were caused by him, or that they were as bad as everyone was claiming, since the stick he'd hit him with was only a switch, even though the witness from whom the stick had been taken referred to it himself as a "staff".[26]

Everything in the incident had been on the part of the teenager, according to exciseman MacLarty, with himself being "violently and wrongly attacked", "stunned", with a lame hand, and bruised and disordered head, which meant that he now had trouble doing his surveying work. He even demanded (in typical MacLarty litigious fashion) that the teenager be transported and his goods confiscated, quoting the 1746 Act of Parliament which specified that any armed assailant who attacked an exciseman within three miles of the sea be charged with felony, without any chance of relying on legal loopholes. It seems however that MacLarty himself was trying to rely on other legal loopholes, as he'd persuaded the Fiscal to demand evidence of the surgeon's fees and a report on the injuries.

This involvement of the Fiscal, at a time when many of the town officials may have been members of respectable local committees, and the way that MacLarty skipped anything worse than a fine after his attack on his sister, tempts one to wonder if he was using his connections to escape such problems. Certainly for someone who'd been involved with riots, fights and quarrels several times, he seems to have only been given fines and those in later years for contravening civil laws. It seems strange that for such a notoriously violent, argumentative man, nothing seems to have been done about his behaviour. If he was a committee member, it must have been acutely uncomfortable for the gentlemen of Campbeltown, feeling obliged to side with a fellow who was fast becoming an embarrassment to them.

In future years, Danny MacLarty's name is strikingly absent from any major altercation mentioned in the old records. There are some of that name in the parish records and one or two in the civil (including a litigious shoemaker with debtors who, curiously, are all sailors[27], or the occasion when Danny contravened the excise act himself[28]) who come before the sheriff or burgh courts, but it may be that his reign of terror over the Campbeltown tax-payers had ended that day on Tayinloan beach. Whether this was because he simply had to change his job after becoming lame in one hand and beaten about the head, or because he left the area for the city or abroad it's not possible to tell. The future of the teenager who'd fought him there on the parchment coloured sands of Tighanloan is doubtful aswell, although one of that name (John Beaton) was marrying in the parish within 14 years.[29]

Could it be then that a teenager had been the one to eventually bring to book such a violent, litigious, bullying character as exciseman MacLarty? With modern policies against bullies in schools, thankfully it would seem that today's Campbeltown teenagers have the opportunity to be just as gutsy when faced with bullies, as young John Beaton was, and although Campbeltown whisky may still bring people into an argument, Askomil appears to be a quieter place without the likes of Danny MacLarty around.

FOOTNOTES

1. "The Whisky Distilleries of the United Kingdom" by Alfred Barnard published David and Charles reprints, 1969, from original print 1887, pp.55-87.
2. Ibid. pp. 81 and 85.
3. Several examples eg. www.smuggling.co.uk or "Smuggling in the British Isles, a history" by R.Platt.
4. E504/8/7 and 6, in the National Records of Scotland, Edinburgh.
5. "The Whisky Distilleries of the United Kingdom" by Alfred Barnard published David and Charles reprints 1969, from original print 1887, p.55; "The Royal Burgh of Inveraray" by Alexander Fraser, published The Saint Andrew Press, 1973, p.113.
6. Several sources eg. "The Campbells of the Ark, men of Argyll", volume 2, by Ronald Black, published John Donald 2017, p.609);

"Kintyre in the 17th century" by A.McKerral, privately published, Edinburgh, 1948, p.138; "Justices of the Peace in Argyll, Processes of the JP Courts, 1674-1825" by Frank Bigwood privately printed 2001, p.31 (this latter may infact be Danny MacLarty himself, working further north than Campbeltown four years after the assault on Jean).
7. SC54/10/5, in the National Records of Scotland, Edinburgh.
8. "The Campbeltown Book", published Kintyre Civic Society, 2003, pp.98,228.
9. The National Library of Scotland, map room website (maps.nls.uk/Scotland/index.html) for General Roy's map, George Langland's map and the 19th century Ordnance Survey maps.
10. SC54/10/5, in the National Records of Scotland, Edinburgh.
11. Ibid.
12. Ibid.
13. Testimony of Dorothy Lumb, 'The Yarnmaker', to whom the author is indebted.
14. SC54/10/5, in the National Records of Scotland, Edinburgh.
15. Ibid; "The Royal Burgh of Inveraray" by Alexander Fraser, published The Saint Andrew Press, 1973, p.16, n.14.
16. "Highland Folkways" by I.F.Grant, published by Routledge and Kegan Paul Ltd, 1975, p.233-5.
17. SC54/10/5, in the National Records of Scotland, Edinburgh.
18. SC54/10/6, in the National Records of Scotland, Edinburgh.
19. Ibid.
20. The National Library of Scotland, map room website (maps.nls.uk/Scotland/index.html) for the Admiralty maps 1849,1851,1867, compared with google maps aerial views.
21. SC54/10/6, in the National Records of Scotland, Edinburgh.
22. Ibid.
23. The National Library of Scotland, map room website (maps.nls.uk/Scotland/index.html) for Admiralty map 1849, George Langlands map.
24. SC54/10/6, in the National Records of Scotland, Edinburgh.
25. Ibid.
26. Ibid.
27. "Campbeltown Court Processes 1752-74, and Deeds 1758-73, by Frank Bigwood, privately printed, p.58.
28. "Justices of the Peace in Argyll, Processes of the JP Courts, 1674-1825" by Frank Bigwood privately printed 2001, pp.69 and 136.
29. The only John Beaton marrying in Campbeltown at a reasonable time would be one who married Flory Weir in 1775 (ref.

scotlandspeople website). As for the future of Jean Stirling she appears to have died in 1774 at the age of 60 years, and is buried in Kilchousland (www.ralstongenealogy.com/brackleygraves. htm).

FOUR

Millions of years ago, layers of clayey, volcanic rock over what is now the west coast of Scotland was changed by the pressures of the earth's movements into greyish layers of a mineral, scattered with quartz and mica.[1] Over the course of time, the land greened over and the mineral eroded out of the crags and cliffs and along the shores, washing up on the beaches or exposed above the water level by the late 17th century, to be gathered locally for building projects. It was only around 1745 that this casual gathering of sea-washed slates was turned into an industry, with quarries first established soon after, and around half a million slates produced annually by crews of men.[2]

By the end of the century, the islands of Easdale, Belnahua, Seil and Luing were turning out five million slates a year[3], with 19 crews of four men each on Luing alone[4], quarrying the mineral from seams above the water level, with the help of horse drawn 'engines', sluices and channels.[5] These quarriers were hardy men, working a punishing day with hand tools and earning their living according to the amount of slates they could produce annually. From the quarry face, where half the crew of men worked, the slate was carried to the other half of the crew, further towards the harbour, to be split into the requisite sizes, ready for shipping to the Clyde and east coast ports. Labourers would be at work around the quarries and slaters, clearing away the rubbish, with the bulk of it invariably going into the sea where it still lies today, occasionally blocking the harbour in a very vigorous swell, and needing clearing to enable the ferry to pull in.[6]

It's been reported that for all their hard won labour, the slate quarriers lived well in comfortable lodgings, with some land, and a wage of one to fifteen shillings per 1,000 slates produced, while a day labourer on the site could earn 9 or 10 pence a day.[7] This was at a time when a day labourer on a farm could earn around a quarter as much again per day.[8]

By the end of the 1700s, the quarries at Easdale were exhausted above water level, although some better equipment would soon be introduced and below water-level quarries dug, while the industry on Luing continued apace.[9] Little Cullipool, now a quiet, picturesque village by a sea-pounded harbour, was a veritable hotbed of industry, people's entire lives touched by the powerhouse that was the Slate industry in Nether Lorn.

The landowner at the time, Campbell of Breadalbane, wasn't it seems the most forgiving of landlords (he once sent an eviction notice to a sick young widow, a week after her husband had died suddenly, stating when she complained, that she could go into service, presumably leaving her two children to be raised by the parish[10]), but he it was who owned some of the best land in Nether Lorn, including a half mile stretch south from Cuan ferry, taking in some fine seashore and excellent pasture land.[11] This croft of Ballacuan (not to be confused with that of the same name over on Seil) was farmed by two men in the closing years of the 1700s. Each had been there for over twenty years, and when, sometime between 1796 and summer 1805, one of them died or vacated their half of the tenancy, the other it seems had gained the entire tack.[12] Obviously with such good land, the remaining tenant, Duncan Marquis (one of the quarriers working for the Slate Company[13]) must have thought all his birthdays had come at once; he hadn't been very happy sharing it with the other man, a ship's captain, anyway.[14] Marquis' satisfaction at getting the whole croft to himself wasn't to last long: a second tenant was given the whole 'sett' in June 1805, and Duncan wasn't at all happy. He managed to get Breadalbane to allow him to retain the byre for a few months, presumably with the excuse that what stock he had on the land still would need to be fed by the grain stored there, and this was allowed him. The new tenant however, would have possession of all the remaining land and buildings, and all the benefits of them.[15]

So it was that Patrick Johnstone, another slate quarrier, took the croft of Ballacuan. Paddy may have been quite a young man, since despite his very local name (there were generations of Johnstones down at Toberonochy until the mid 19th century[16]), he only comes on record as being over 18 years old in 1803, when he was listed as possible volunteer material for the militia.[17] He was working at the quarries on Luing at the time, and clearly he didn't get called up to be a soldier, since one morning in June 1805, he was met with an unusual sight as he arrived back at Ballacuan. He may have gone down to the ferry quite early for some reason, since it was between nine and ten when he arrived back at the farm. There in his paddock, was a group of strange horses. Presumably he found out from someone close by that they belonged to some tenants of Breadalbane, and their owners were on their way to pay their rents on Seil, and had left the animals there overnight, paying a fee to Duncan Marquis, as part of the deal.[18]

Paddy Johnstone, naturally, was somewhat put out by this turn of events, and set off to find Marquis to demand the money which hadn't been his to charge the travellers. Up the slope from the paddock and the horses, was the byre, supposedly kept by Duncan for storing feed for his remaining stock before he vacated his share of the tenancy completely.

For a building which was supposed to be just a byre however, there were an unusual number of men going in and out of it, and Paddy knew that Duncan had also converted the building into a dwelling house for himself, his wife and his ten year old daughter.

When Paddy entered this 'byre', he found it not just holding animal feed and a temporary dwelling for the Marquises, but a whole lot more besides. Duncan had converted the place into a pub (the slate-built partition which may have divided the public section of the building from the families bedroom, still exists), and he was in bed there, half-dressed and the worse for drink.[19] With him in the bed was his daughter; the section where the beds would have been is easily large enough to accommodate two, and although several people sleeping in one bed wasn't unusual in those days,[20] for a family of only three people, with plenty of room for two beds, it seems rather strange. Amusingly, the clerk who wrote the account in the old records of how Duncan Marquis was half dressed and in bed, had a problem writing the word "trousers"– had he been more used to writing "breeks" before now?[21]

On seeing his neighbour, and now successor in the tenancy, enter the byre/pub, Duncan Marquis became angry, and got out of bed, shouting at him, accusing him of being a thief and grabbing the tongs from the fire (probably in the middle of the floor) to hit the younger man with. Paddy managed to wrestle the tongs off him, and the two men argued noisily, threatening each other, and attracting the attention of some of the neighbours, or the men who'd left their horses in the paddock. One of them advised Paddy not to bother with Duncan, clearly trying to placate the situation, but the former declared he wouldn't allow himself to be called a thief, and they took the argument outdoors. Paddy's cottage was only a few yards from the byre doorway, and since Duncan it seems had only recently converted the byre into a dwelling and pub, there must have been a few spare slates lying around. Paddy clearly had his back turned to Duncan at one point, and despite probably being twice Paddy's age, the older man managed, in his semi-drunken state, to lift a slate heavy enough to do some damage. This in itself tells of the strength of the old slate quarriers, as any piece big enough to do such damage is heavier than it looks.

With the older man lifting a slate as a weapon behind him, it was only the warning shout from two of the neighbours, which alerted Paddy as to what being was aimed at his head, and he turned round in time to prevent himself being hit by the slate. Quite how the argument ended isn't stated in the trial notes, but the younger man did manage to get the slate off Duncan, and presumably the pair of them were induced to go back into their respective dwellings.

Duncan Marquis' temper however was still simmering. He evidently still considered the whole tenancy as his and was acting as if it was, renting out the paddock to travellers, and running a pub from the byre. Incensed by the altercation, and by the challenge to what he still considered his tenancy, later that same day Duncan and his wife lodged a complaint against Paddy with Breadalbane's factor at Clachan on Seil. Paddy was subsequently called up to give a statement to the factor, and the pair were advised to live in good neighbourliness with each other in future, or at least presumably until Duncan's tenancy ran out. Mild words indeed, and it seems that Paddy made a good effort at taking the advice by simply not visiting Duncan, going near him or his family, or tangling with them again.

As for Duncan Marquis, his pub business was thriving it appears and despite being described in the records as "frail and weakly" (in itself probably a lie, if he was strong enough to lift a slate to use as a weapon), he and his wife spent a few days after the argument travelling the district on foot buying spirits to sell in the pub, perhaps leaving the place to be held together by their ten year old daughter. By the Monday after the argument, Duncan was so exhausted from the travelling (and from more drinking of the profits probably!) that he took to his bed. He didn't leave it alive, dying three weeks later, still "much addicted to alcohol".

With the bread-winner gone, and perhaps thinking on the outcome from the other tenant's widow who'd been forced into service, Duncan's wife appealed to the factor again, accusing Paddy Johnstone of murder.

It took until October for the trial to come to court, and with the previous good behaviour of young Paddy Johnstone, he was perhaps permitted to stay at home after his arrest (nearly three weeks after Duncan's death), under the caution of Breadalbane's factor, until the time came for him to attend court.[22]

The surrounds of the Inveraray tolbooth had changed quite a bit since the day when the farmer from Acharacle had dumped his disabled son on the Sheriff's doorstep in 1761. The great imposing building facing the loch, with its bottom storey gaol and the corridor where the prisoners were walked to the view of passing locals, was still as imposing. Now however, the hotel the other side of the avenue had stables behind it,[23] a house had been built for the Duke's chamberlain matching that of the Sheriff on the opposite side of the tolbooth and the avenue was arched over by white painted screens.[24] Infact the whole frontage of Sheriff's house, tolbooth, Chamberlain's house, screen and hotel was white painted and so impressive from up the road, that it was mistaken at least once for the castle, and would be recognisable to modern visitors.[25] The other side of Front street was equally recognisable, with the manses and the house with the turnpike stair at the back, while the pier had at last been built, and extended twice.[26]

Behind Front street, the tenements either side of Main street, were divided into East and West by a fine double church with a steeple, and although the roads and lanes were largely unpaved, and the buildings for the common people already becoming dilapidated with several unofficial middens (despite two proper ones), roaming farm animals, and no nice white paint for the walls,[27] the people (over a thousand of them in the town itself[28]) were noted as being generous, brave, humane and peaceable, although too susceptible to alcohol for the taste of the minister.[29] The fishing industry was thriving, with fish remnants, boats and nets scattered all along the shore, not exactly a pretty sight to the numerous high-class visitors who approached the town along the fine new military road and the bridge adjoining the burial ground, again a familiar sight to many modern visitors.[30]

The Duke's efforts at establishing a woollen industry in the town had failed spectacularly, but the other traders and small businesses usually did a roaring trade with the visitors, even outside of market days or the visits of the high court.[31]

The argument between Paddy Johnstone and Duncan Marquis had happened around the 19th June, with Duncan dying on the 9th July. By the end of August, the Inveraray surgeon had made his statement, and the trial (the court having travelled from Edinburgh) began nearly six weeks later,[32] infront of one Baronet James Montgomery (a name not unfamiliar to Kintyre residents a century earlier!) a rich nobleman from Tweeddale with extensive inherited land and property and a London barrister for a brother. Clearly a wise and careful man where his money was concerned, he wasn't ungenerous, and was happy to acknowledge loyalty and hard work in his employees. He was in his forties at the time, but was newly married to the daughter of the Earl of Selkirk, and due to have a large and happy family in future years.[33]

Before this veritable pillar of Scottish justice, Paddy Johnstone, the quarrier and crofter from Ballacuan, stood accused of 'hamesucken' (breaking into someone's home and beating them up[34]) aswell as murder. Such an accusation from the widow of a small tenant in rural Argyll, was truly something to have to live up to, and the charge which Paddy heard as he stood in the court room of the tolbooth in Inveraray, must have been daunting to his ears. He was accused of having "deadly hatred, malice and ill will" towards Duncan Marquis, whom he "barbarously and wickedly and feloniously bruised and assaulted".[35]

The witnesses were his neighbours from Ballacuan, some of the men who'd brought their horses to the paddock that fateful morning and perhaps the people who'd seen Duncan Marquis, hale and hearty (if still inebriated!) in the days after the argument. Also included on the list, for formal necessity, is the jailor at Inveraray (a sign of the times: the old spelling of 'gaoler' and 'gaol' seems to be abandoned around this time), and the surgeon who'd probably attended on Duncan before his death, or had conducted the post-mortem. Curiously, heading the list of witnesses are two names, one perhaps for the defence (an upstanding figure of the community, whose statement would be believed above all others), the other for the prosecution: Duncan's own daughter, little Nancy Marquis, biased maybe, but her innocence undoubtedly being relied on by the prosecution.

As far as the accusation of murder was concerned however, none of the adult witnesses appeared to be speaking against Paddy, and he seems to have been the model prisoner, calmly telling the truth and not changing his statement in panic or pushing for the use of legal loopholes. Some of the names on the jury are recognisable to Argyll historians (the two Stevenson merchants from Oban, or MacDougall gentrymen from Knipoch and Lunga) along with farmers, tradesmen and craftsmen from Dalmally, Kilbrandon, Inveraray and even Kilmartin parishes.

It took only three days for Paddy's fate to be examined and decided upon by this jury. For some reason James Montgomery wasn't in the judgement seat at the sentencing, his place being taken by Lord Nairn of Dunsinnan, but this doesn't seem to have affected the outcome of the trial.[36]

The hamesucken accusation against Paddy Johnstone in Ballacuan was upheld, but with only an arbitrary sentence, probably a fine, or perhaps he'd already served the equivalent during what little jail-term he served before the trial. As for the murder accusation, the verdict came back a resounding Not Proven. Paddy was "assoilzed and dismissed from the bar" and allowed to return to Luing a free man, perhaps bowed down by his experience, and certainly making no friends with widow Marquis presumably still living in the byre-cum–pub-cum-cottage next door, but having the support of his other neighbours at Ballacuan.[37]

When each family ended their tenancies on Luing isn't clear. With the former attitude of Lord Breadalbane to a crofter's widow, it's likely that Duncan's wife and daughter weren't allowed to stay. Although there are some families of the Marquis name in the parish, and beyond, there isn't any record of Duncan's death, or of a headstone, and young Nancy's marriage, or her mother's re–marriage are also untraceable. As for Paddy Johnstone, perhaps he took another tenancy away from Luing (Breadalbane had other lands eg.out at Dalmally), or perhaps he moved up to Ballachulish for the slate quarrying work there, in order to leave the whole memory of the incident behind him.[38]

The site of Duncan and Paddy's altercation, and the lively (or slightly suspicious, where little Nancy was concerned) scene at the byre/pub there, are now scattered remnants of walls, sheep fanks, old tracks and piles of slates that were once busy crowded cottages. The locally famous rich pastures of Ballacuan still stretch down to Cuan ferry, the rigs and furrows of the land now studded with daisies in spring, while the bluffs and crags bloom with primroses and look out on a scene so quiet and so idyllic that it's almost surreal.

From the green pastures of Ballacuan, the rocky forms of the land above Ellanabeich across the water, and the white clusters of cottages there seem totally different now to the grinding and crashing hive of industry which it once was, the grey dust of the slate clouding the scene where now only sea mist obscures the view of the distant hills of Mull.

Over on Seil and Easdale, and down at Cullipool, the Slate Industry has long gone, but history always has a way of re-emerging, and in the work of the local history society on Luing and in the enlightening little museum on Seil, and other museums and heritage centres on the islands, the memory of those hardy people who earned a tough living extracting an ancient mineral from the hillsides is now preserved. Long may it be so.

FOOTNOTES

1. "Encyclopaedia Britannica, micro/macropaedia, volume IX, published Helen Meningway Benton, 1973-4, p.265.
2. "Royal Commission on Ancient and Historical Monuments of Scotland", Argyll, volume 2, Lorn, published 974, p.279
3. "The Second Statistical Account", volume 7, Renfrewshire and Argyll, published Blackwood and Sons, Edinburgh, 1845, p.78.

4. "Royal Commission on Ancient and Historical Monuments of Scotland", Argyll, volume 2, Lorn, published 1974, p.279 (Seil itself at this early date being separate from Ellenabeich, and not therefore grouped in with the 5 crews there and the 13 on Easdale).
5. "The Second Statistical Account", volume 7, Renfrewshire and Argyll, published Blackwood and Sons, Edinburgh, 1845, p.78; "Royal Commission on Ancient and Historical Monuments of Scotland", Argyll, volume 2, Lorn, published 1974, p.278-9.
6. The Slate Islands Trust museum, Ellanbeich, Seil.
7. "The First Statistical Account" volume XX, c.1792, p.174-5; "The Second Statistical Account", volume 7, Renfrewshire and Argyll, published Blackwood and Sons, Edinburgh, 1845, p.78.
8. "The First Statistical Account" volume XX, c.1792, p.79,90,104.
9. "Royal Commission on Ancient and Historical Monuments of Scotland", Argyll, volume 2, Lorn, published 1974, p.279.
10. FH206 at Argyll & Bute County archives ("Live Argyll"), Manse Brae, Lochgilphead.
11. Ibid.
12. Ibid; JC13/34f/27v; JC26/1805/18 in the National Records of Scotland, Edinburgh.
13. JC13/34f/27v; JC26/1805/18 in the National Records of Scotland, Edinburgh.
14. FH206 at Argyll & Bute County archives ("Live Argyll"), Manse Brae, Lochgilphead.
15. JC13/34f/27v; JC26/1805/18 in the National Records of Scotland, Edinburgh.
16. The author's copy (taken down personally on a site visit) of the Monumental Inscriptions of Luing burial ground. Similar details are available at Argyll & Bute County Archives ("Live Argyll"), Manse Brae, Lochgilphead.
17. Militia Men lists, 1804, Kilbrandon parish, available at Argyll & Bute County Archives ("Live Argyll"), Manse Brae, Lochgilphead.
18. JC13/34f/27v;JC26/1805/18 in the National Records of Scotland, Edinburgh.
19. Ibid.
20. Several sources eg."History Revealed" magazine, September 2018, p.73.
21. JC13/34f/27v; JC26/1805/18 in the National Records of Scotland, Edinburgh.
22. Ibid.
23. Inv&Dks pp.261,266.
24. Ibid., pp.266,270.

25. Ibid., p.271.
26. Ibid., p.266
27. Inv&Dks 271, 286-88.
28. "The First Statistical Account" volume XX, c.1792, p,142.
29. Ibid., p.157; Inv&Dks, p.279.
30. Ibid. ; Inv & Dks, p.142.
31. Ibid., p.140; Inv&Dks, p.273,272, 294-5.
32. JC13/34f/27v; JC26/1805/18 in the National Records of Scotland, Edinburgh.
33. Inv&Dks p.337; scotlands people website re.wills, marriages and deaths. Interestingly, Sir James not only left his family well provided for at his death, but £100 to his butler, £20 each to his coachman, footman and carter and a £10 p.a. pension to his gamekeeper and overseer, or their respective widows.
34. "Scots Theasaurus" edited by Iseabail Macleod, published Polygon, Edinburgh, 1999, p.266.
35. JC13/34f/27v; JC26/1805/18 in the National Records of Scotland, Edinburgh.
36. Ibid.
37. Ibid.
38. There appear to have been a few Johnstones in Ballachulish parish in later decades (ref.the 1841 census parish of Lismore and Appin (Duror, Ballachulish and Glencoe), books 15,19 and 20, pages 2 and 12 for Duror, Inverco, and Kinlochleven cottages). There are several Marquises lying in the burial ground on Luing, but none that obviously tie in with young Nancy or her mother.

FIVE

In the early years of the 1800s, the economy in Argyll was taking a nose dive. With taxes soaring to help pay for recent wars, and the prices of basic necessities rising to cover the producers' expenses on the taxes, whatever legal or illegal way out the rural dwellers could find to supplement their income, they took. Being a coastal county of course, smuggling was one of those ways out, and with smuggling, came illegal distilling, and with illegal distilling and smuggling, came the notorious excisemen, such as Danny MacLarty a generation earlier.[1]

It was perhaps an innkeeper at the village of Kilmichael Glassary who tipped off the local exciseman about one of his fellow hostlers one late November day in 1804. The whistleblower may have been Duncan Barr who held the inn on the site of the property now known as 'High Building',[2] while one could imagine the competition he had from Angus Leitch who had the tenancy of the changehouse over the road. Duncan had probably long known of the illegal activities going on in the fields above the changehouse, and maybe it was a personal vendetta between the two men and their families which gave Duncan cause to inform on his neighbour. Whatever the circumstances beforehand, exciseman Alex MacDonald arrived at Glassary with some assistants one Monday morning, and approached a small building just over a rise from the changehouse.[3]

Alex was certainly a tough, capable and active man and he may have come to Kilmichael via an old track between his home at Rudill and the hill above the village.[4]

Half-hidden by the rise of the land above the changehouse, and further disguised as a corn byre[5](and perhaps even used as such in the years before and afterwards), the small building which exciseman MacDonald had come to investigate now housed the makings of quite an efficient little illicit whisky-still. Entering this 'corn' byre, Alex found not only the equipment, in use and ready for the taking, but a woman who may have been Angus Leitch's wife, and the mother of at least one of his sons. Angus had had an illegitimate son to another woman in the village before he'd married Sarah, and that boy was now in his late teens, and happened to be in the vicinity at the time of the exciseman's visit.

Doubtless delighted that he'd caught the illegal distillers red-handed, Alex MacDonald announced to the woman that he was going to seize the equipment, at which she promptly started screaming blue murder – quite literally, as the old records say she shouted "Murder!". At that, and from all angles and almost every cottage doorway, the people of Kilmichael rushed out to the still-house, and, led by Donald Leitch, started beating up the exciseman and his assistants, before dragging them out of the structure, and down the hill to Duncan Barr's house. Here, Alex MacDonald was eventually able to free himself from the grip of the mob, and ran back to the still-house. Diving within, he tried to secure the door, but it was forced open by Donald Leitch, armed with stones and rocks, which he proceeded to throw at the exciseman.[6]

At that time, the current road at Kilmichael, going past the inn (now The Old Horseshoe Inn) and joining the modern road 200yds south, had not long been built, although the bridge was rather older.[7] The road infact seems to have been one of the ones in mid Lorn which required constant upkeep[8], while winding up away from it, were the early versions, again not long built, of the stone walls which now criss-cross so many an Argyll hillside.[9] One of these walls, now much ruined and barely traceable in places, infact runs fairly close to the ruins of the illegal still-house,[10] and it may well have been from this recently built wall that Donald Leitch and the other Kilmichael men picked their weapons to start stoning the poor exciseman and his assistants. Alex was actually hit badly in the head with one stone, and eventually had to retire himself and his party to the shelter of Duncan Barr's inn, the door nevertheless being pelted with rocks and stones for quite a while afterwards. The fact that Alex gained shelter at the Barrs, would indicate that Duncan wasn't part of the band which was attached to the illegal distilling operation, and there were clearly others in the village who were on the side of law and order, as Alex sent out for help to the local Argyll Volunteers, headed by surgeon MacArthur as ensign.[11]

Later the same day, with darkness having meanwhile fallen, Ensign MacArthur, with a band of armed volunteer soldiery including one Sergeant MacKellar, assembled at the door of Duncan Barr's inn to accompany the excise and his assistants back to the wee still-house. Also assembled there (someone had obviously tipped them off!) was the stone-wielding riot mob, and the attacks resumed with the same ferocity as before. Exciseman MacDonald persisted however, and, protected by the soldiers firing muskets, he entered the still-house to find the bigger equipment gone. Vats, pipework, barrels, and all, had disappeared, perhaps over the hill towards Balliemore, along the track ironically which Alex may have taken himself in order to sneak up on the distillers.[12] All that was left were a few small utensils, so Alex and his men started gathering those up instead, probably thinking that with the soldiers at the door they were safe from the mob.[13]

Even today the ruins of the still-house sits with its rear wall half-built in the slope of the hill behind it, and the thatched roof[14] would have been easily accessible from this direction. While the exciseman was busy collecting the smaller equipment, young Dougie Leitch, Donald's (legitimate) half brother and only 12 or 13 years old[15], clambered through a hole in the thatch and started repeating his sibling's assault, while outside, the mob resumed their stone–throwing at the soldiers. This mob was made of strong, working rural men, used to handling heavy tools, shoving recalcitrant cows around and building and repairing their own walls, cottages and roads – then drinking the evening away on Angus Leitch's illicit whisky! The soldiers the mob were attacking were their neighbours and friends, equally tough and used to hard work and hard fighting. Small wonder then that with such combatants, Sgt MacKellar was badly injured in the head, there were further incitements to attack the excise, and Alex and his assistants were forced to abandon the job and come out from the still-house. It was only with "considerable difficulty" however that they managed to retreat again to the safety of Duncan Barr's inn, where they spent the rest of the night, guarded by the soldiery outside. The following morning, perhaps thinking that the excise were going to return to the still-house, the mob was waiting for them, but Alex had given up the effort as a bad job, and he left it to the authorities to bring the Leitch boys, as leaders of the assault, to justice.[16]

With the winter weather making communications and travel (even with the fine new roads in mid Lorn)[17] difficult, there's no wonder it took until the middle of January for Donnie and Dougie Leitch to appear in Inveraray tolbooth, (accompanied by their brother John who was also included in the charges).[18] In classic fashion for this criminal family, the messenger sent from town to leave the summons in their hands, couldn't find them, so he returned to Inveraray and left it, as was the custom, attached to the door of the tolbooth (the mercat cross, lost when the old town was replaced by the new town, still hadn't been found).[19]

After being examined before Sheriff substitute Duncan Campbell, the Leitch boys were permitted, under caution and with someone standing surety for them, to return to Kilmichael in the meantime, and it seems the surety worked, as they pitched up again at Inveraray when the circuit court returned to the town in May.[20]

Standing in the dock at the tolbooth, and infront of the same Advocate James Montgomery who would try Paddy Johnstone from Luing later that year, Donnie Leitch used the typical Argyll criminal's reasoning when faced with the charges: he denied all involvement with the mob, denied ever having even handled a rock in assault, and had infact been in his friend's house that day when he heard the commotion outside, and saw the militia firing. He'd seen some rocks thrown at the exciseman, but didn't know who threw them (certainly not him!), and infact he didn't see exciseman MacDonald injured by the mob in any way.

Clearly neither the jury, nor Advocate Montgomery believed Donnie's statement and the verdict for the pair of them was clear – both were thoroughly guilty, while their other brother, John, was fully acquitted.

At this period, and it seems in Argyll at least, prison terms were just being introduced as a punishment in themselves. Whilst not completely true that time behind bars had previously only been a convenient way of keeping hold of a criminal until his real sentence could be enacted (whether transportation, hanging, flogging or a hefty fine), the Inveraray court up until this era certainly seems to have withheld custodial sentences.[21] The Leitch boys therefore may have assumed that a fine was on their way, which of course they couldn't pay. James Montgomery however gave the boys another sentence – four months behind bars for Donnie, and three months for young Dougie.[22]

Curiously, Angus, their father wasn't prosecuted at all, even though the still–house was declared to have been his. The answer to this engima may come later, with Angus' future occupation.

Four months after Donnie Leitch, the changehouse keeper's (illegitimate) son at Kilmichael was confined in the Inveraray tolbooth, he returned home to his mother's house. He wasn't away from the tolbooth for long however. Just six months later he broke open a padlock on a byre at Bailliemore, and found there a chest containing, amongst other things, a pocket book. Within the wee book was, for Donnie Leitch, treasure: some IOUs which he could cash in, a couple of invoices, which he could similarly claim the money on, and a receipt for a watch left at John Ross, the watch repairers in Inveraray, which he could now go and collect, then presumably sell. It's not stated in the Sheriff records how anyone knew it was Donnie who'd stolen the pocket book and its contents, so perhaps someone saw him, or he boasted about it later, or (more likely) he went into Inveraray to pick up the repaired watch, and a suspicious Ross told the authorities there. Whoever it was who'd 'clyped' on Donnie, he was up before the Sheriff again within a few days, pleading guilty at first, then later changing his statement, saying that he'd been drunk when he made the first statement, and under the impression that he'd get an easier sentence if he confessed early on. The second time around he said that although he'd broken into the byre and taken the pocket book, he later burnt it and the contents without opening it, and had returned home to his mum's house that night without venturing forth again.[23]

With another guilty verdict, one would have expected the sentence to be more harsh for Donnie Leitch this time round, and Donnie himself perhaps expected it. He was to be fined 100 marks, which, like with the still-house attack, he clearly couldn't pay, but he suggested an alternative himself. Occasionally after being convicted, a young man's sentence would be to serve in the military or the navy, and Donnie Leitch may have assumed that time serving in uniform would be a natural choice for him, and he stated so. He was willing to join the military. Was he perhaps hoping for a life of excitement with weapons and more fighting, perhaps having been refused admission into the Argyll Volunteers because of his criminal past, but impressed by their conduct on the night of the still-house attack?[24]

Sheriff Campbell perhaps agreed to this alternative, since the teenage thief from Kilmichael disappears from the old Argyll records for some time, leaving the scene open for his younger brother and his dad.

Angus was in his early fifties by then[25], and it must have been soon after the still-house attack and Donnie's theft from Bailliemore, that the family left Kilmichael. With the rising importance of Lochgilphead, it seems that the Leitch's changehouse was decommissioned, perhaps even demolished and the site rebuilt on.[26] In town, Angus was on the search for a job, and ironically he seems to have turned up on the excise's doorstep, and succeeded in getting himself a minor role in the institution.[27] One day in early summer, he and his boss and a colleague (curiously by the surname MacLarty!) intercepted a local farm worker conveying some sacks of malt to another field locally, but without the necessary pass for such work. To prevent the self-same illicit distilling which Angus had been part of a few years before, such passes were imposed on farmers who had a load of malt to convey somewhere, to avoid it being conveyed to an illicit still. On this occasion, the three excisemen confiscated the sacks of malt, four horses and presumably the wagon they were pulling, and took the lot to town for safe keeping, depositing them in the changehouse there. The farm worker was given the appropriate paperwork to show his boss (one of the horses was his own however), and which he could use to retrieve the animals, on payment of a fee, to ensure that he returned them to custody when demanded and when the case came to court. This he duly did, leaving some £28 in Angus Leitch's hands.[28]

This of course was far from the end of the matter, as within a few days, a certain Dougie Leitch turned up at the farm with a note from the authorities (as if!) demanding the return of the horses so they could be sold to pay the fine associated with the case. The farm worker had no option but to comply, but he must have had some doubts about the issue, because he went back to town without any horses, only determining to sort it all out once and for all. He was right to be doubtful. The old records are quite confusing at this stage, with several different accounts being offered, not all of them clearly written, let alone dated, but it seems as though Angus Leitch had the cost of the horses in mind, had tried to fool some JPs into signing dodgy paperwork (one of them was taken in), the senior excise officer being wise to Angus' tricks but not doing much to prevent it, and the farm-worker trying to get written witness statements to support his side of argument. In the end, Angus Leitch refused to hand back the £28 (he denied all knowledge of it!), the farmer got his horses back (though the farm-worker's one had already been sold), and the JPs were satisfied, if annoyed.[29]

Less than a year later, the Leitch family came to the attention of the Inveraray courts yet again. This time, young Dougie, now all grown up and in his early twenties, stole 11 yards of linen from a hostler and his wife in Lochgilphead, taking the fabric straight to one Anne Gordon in the town, and asking her to make some shirts for him out of it. Anne must have done something with the linen, as when Dougie came to pick up his newly-made shirts, he found there was rather less than 11 yards there, and no shirts. Had she thieved from the thief? All Dougie could do however at that point was take the fabric to someone else, this time widow MacLarty back at their old haunts of Glassary, where the hostler and his wife eventually tracked down 6½ yards of their linen (identifiable from an iron-mould mark on the fibres). That same day, the hostler had visitors at his establishment in Lochgilphead: Angus and Dougie turned up on the doorstep, and proceeded to beat and assault both the hostler and his wife "to the great effusion of blood and danger of life", in revenge for the restitution of the linen. This time, Angus Leitch was in the dock with his son, and they were both found guilty, and fined £30 sterling. They even had the Leitch family downright cheek to apply for bail, which, surprisingly, they got.[30]

It's at this point that Dougie Leitch's story becomes rather convoluted. Two years after being convicted of beating up the Lochgilphead hostler who'd retrieved his stolen linen, one Dugald Leitch, a known and notorious thief, was apprehended in Stirling on the charge of stealing a pocket watch from someone in Glasgow. He still had the remains of the watch on him when he was caught, and after his trial he was sentenced to seven years transportation, a sentence from which it was rare for anyone to return home.[31] Nine years later however, another Dougie Leitch (or was it the same one, having returned from transportation?), and this time definitely Angus' son from Lochgilphead, broke into an outhouse in the town. His father had owed a debt to a family in Edinburgh, and, having not paid his dues, the Edinburgh folk took him to court, and Angus Leitch's house at Dunmore was emptied of various furniture and fittings with the intention of selling them to pay off the debt. Until the time came for the sale, the items were stored in the outhouse belonging to a Lochgilphead vintner, only to become the target of a break-in. Back the furniture went to Angus' house, from where they were collected again by the courts and lodged (for greater security) with a clerk of court.[32] Angus Leitch's furniture may have been tracked down and confiscated again, but Dougie Leitch was nowhere to be seen; not unusual for that family, and notice of his outlawry was posted at Inveraray. It took the authorities five years to track him down, and, at last behind bars, Dougie Leitch appealed for bail. Who on earth thought that a man who was such a hardened thief and had recently gone outlaw, was the ideal candidate for bail, is anyone's guess, but it's not difficult to think what happened next. Off Dougie went, an outlaw again, being picked up sooner this time, after only a couple of months, and securely behind Inveraray bars again, his later history in doubt, due to lack of detailed records at that point.[33]

Curiously however, the Dougie Leitch who'd been convicted in Stirling of stealing the pocket watch, was back in Scotland again the same year that the Argyll Dougie was last on record as being in jail in Inveraray. It truly seems as though the two men may be one and the same, the Stirling Dougie also being convicted of housebreaking and theft that same year.[34]

The saga of the criminal family of Leitches from Kilmichael and Lochgilphead appears to peter out after this. A Hugh Leitch spent twelve months in Inveraray jail in future years, but he was a first-time criminal, and doesn't seem to have come to the court's attention again,[35] whilst in 1841, old Angus and his wife were still alive and living in Lochgilphead, with a relative called Dugald, although the latter was rather younger than his notorious son should have been.[36] A year later, one Dugald Leitch arrived in the USA from Scotland on the ship 'American', and within a few years, old Angus and his wife probably died.[37]

It's ironic that, just like the problem the courts had at the time pinning down the well-known but slippery customers whom the Leitches were, any historian who tries to track the family down in the old records, finds the surname mentioned almost everywhere – but can never truly track down their eventual fates. Perhaps the final word can be left to an old gentleman who died at his home in Glassary parish in 1865. His name was Donald Leitch, and he was the same approximate age as the young man who'd been convicted of the attack on exciseman MacDonald and of thieving the pocket book, way back in the early years of the century, and who had offered to join the military as punishment. However this old gentleman said his father was not an Angus, but a John.[38]

With no other likely Donald Leitch of similar age being noted in the Glassary area at that time, and with the strictures of Victorian society on illegitimate-born people (even respectable grocers and post-masters such as this old gentleman), was he trying to escape his criminal past? If he was, it's only a tribute to himself, as he'd clearly turned his life around, possibly with the help of military discipline, unlike his younger brother. One does wonder however, if, sometime after 1842, a certain Scot by the surname of Leitch became known to the courts in America!

FOOTNOTES

1. Several sources eg. "The First Statistical Account" volume XX, c.1792, pp.4,5,83-84,108,176,190 etc.
2. The author's own conclusion drawn from lengthy study of various old maps in The National Library of Scotland, available on the map room website (maps.nls.uk/Scotland/index.html), especially General Roys c. 1750, George Langlands c.1803, and the early Ordnance Survey the latter of which especially strongly indicate a building on this site. In the original trial records, the still-house is quoted as being uphill from Duncan Barr's inn, and the other substantial building in the immediate area being the one on the site of the current primary school, which due to the closeness of the still-house is likely to have been the Leitches changehouse. This also ties in with the future occasion of the Leitches moving away to Lochgilphead (see note 26) at the time the first school on this site was built, while there were clearly Barrs living in the immediate vicinity at the time of the early census records.
3. JC13/34f,20r; JC26/1805/15 in the National Records of Scotland, Edinburgh.
4. scotlandspeople website re.baptismal records.
5. See note 10.
6. JC13/34f,20r; JC26/1805/15 in the National Records of Scotland, Edinburgh.
7. "The First Statistical Account" volume XX, c.1792, p.107-8; Inventory no.7, pp.505-6 (bridge dated 1737).
8. "The First Statistical Account" volume XX, c.1792, pp.107-8,118-9; various occasions in the Minutes of the Roads Trustees, available at Argyll & Bute County Archives ("Live Argyll"), Manse Brae, Lochgilphead.
9. Various sources including "The First Statistical Account" volume XX, c.1792, pp.xxiv,102,199 etc.
10. The author's own site research (spring 2019) and personal experience locating and identifying corn kilns, byres and

abandoned dwellings in Lorn. The old maps (mainly General Roys, George Langlands and the early OS in The National Library of Scotland, map room website (maps.nls.uk/Scotland/index.html)) covering the immediate vicinity of the changehouse at Glassary indicate two possibilities for the still-house/corn byre amongst the smaller structures extant at the time. One of these is now almost untraceable, being very close to the current road and even in 1804 far too close to the changehouse to be the likely spot. The second site is just over a rise, and would have been invisible from the road and the lower stories of the changehouse, except for the smoke or the ridge of its roof. This therefore is a far more likely site for a secret still. Corn byres fit the necessities of a still-house admirably, since rising smoke, someone in attendance all day, and loads of grain being conveyed to the site wouldn't be suspicious, but are also the activity of a still–house. The remains of this other structure have an obvious flue and a cell on the end of the building, although the original structure may have been a dwelling, later converted to a byre, then the still-house. See also "The Whisky Distilleries of the United Kingdom" by Alfred Barnard, published by David & Charles Reprints, 1969, from an original print of 1887, the Introduction (pages un-numbered).
11. JC13/34f; JC26/1805/15 in the National Records of Scotland, Edinburgh.
12. Ibid.
13. Ibid.
14. "Highland Folkways" by I.F.Grant, published by Routledge and Kegan Paul Ltd, 1975 p.147.
15. JC13/34f,20r; JC26/1805/15 in the National Records of Scotland, Edinburgh.
16. Ibid.
17. "The First Statistical Account" volume XX, c.1792, pp.107-8,118-9; Various mentions in the Minutes of the Road Trustees, available at Argyll & Bute Archives ("Live Argyll"), Manse Brae, Lochgilphead.
18. JC13/34f,20r; JC26/1805/15 in the National Records of Scotland, Edinburgh.
19. "The Royal Burgh of Inveraray" by Alexander Fraser, published The Saint Andrew Press, 1973, p.41.
20. JC13/34f,20r; JC26/1805/15 in the National Records of Scotland, Edinburgh.
21. Several sources eg."The Story of Crime and Punishment" (BBC History magazine special), edited by Charlotte Hodgman,

published Immediate Media Company, Bristol, 2018; "The Argyll Justiciary records, volume II 1705-1742, published by the Stair Society, Edinburgh, 1969, p.XVII; "Shades of the Prison House" by H.Potter, published The Boydell Press Ltd, Suffolk, 2019, pp.3,14-15 and 45.

22. JC13/34f,20r; JC26/1805/15 in the National Records of Scotland, Edinburgh.
23. JC26/1806/19 in the National Records of Scotland, Edinburgh.
24. JC13/34f,20r; JC26/1805/15 in the National Records of Scotland, Edinburgh; "The Argyll Justiciary records, volume II 1705-1742, published by the Stair Society, Edinburgh, 1969, pp.203,260.
25. The 1841 census return, Lochgilphead, Glassary parish, on the scotlandspeople website.
26. The National Library of Scotland, map room website (maps.nls.uk/Scotland/index.html) for the change of use of the site, to a school, and complete reordering of the buildings on the spot. See also note 2.
27. AD14/15/10, JC 26/1829/143 in the National Records of Scotland, Edinburgh.
28. AD14/15/10 in the National Records of Scotland, Edinburgh.
29. Ibid.
30. SC54/10/13, AD14/15/28 in the National Records of Scotland, Edinburgh.
31. JC26/1820/133; JC13/47 in the National Records of Scotland, Edinburgh.
32. JC26/1829/143,; JC8/34/81 in the National Records of Scotland,Edinburgh.
33. Ibid.
34. HH21/35/1, JC26/1835/386, in the National Records of Scotland, Edinburgh.
35. HH21/35/1 in the National Records of Scotland, Edinburgh.
36. 1841 census return for Lochgilphead, Glassary parish, on the scotlandspeople website.
37. scotlandspeople website, for the Dougie Leitch who emigrated to the USA on the ship "American" in 1842; the 1851 census return for Lochgilphead, Glassary parish, and any other parish in Scotland which failed to turn up any reference to an Angus Leitch of the approximate age .
38. Death certificate of a Donald Leitch, postmaster and grocer, who died in December 1865 at Ederline in Glassary parish, at the age 82. The person who registered his death stated that his father was a John Leitch (this latter information available on the scotlandspeople website). There was another elderly Donald

Leitch who died around the same time, but in Glenorchy parish, with parents from that district, and a Donald Leitch (no age specified) who was present at an alleged murder on Loch Fyne c.1829, but the postmaster and grocer appears to be the only one of the approximate age and living in the appropriate district.

SIX

With Argyll being a rural county with an enormous coastline, it's unsurprising that water (salt or fresh) has always played a significant part in the county's criminal history. Murderers, thieves and other criminals have used the power of water to kill or maim, they've escaped by sea (or been aiming to), or have deposited their victims off the coast or in lochs. Tides have carried criminals across water, or thieves moved about by boat, they've attacked their victims on shipboard, or ultimately been conveyed to Inveraray by sea, following their apprehension. There've been criminal disputes associated with ferries, or witches accused of causing a shipwreck, while one criminal gang even had their HQ in the middle of a lochan. Stolen goods have been hidden underwater or beside water, and one killer was prevented from being hanged at the appointed place, due to flooded rivers and a wayward tide. Whether at an abandoned farmstead, now unused field, or still populous town, water has played such an important part in Argyll's criminal history that it's not surprising that for the last two murderers hanged in the county, water played a significant part in their crimes.[1]

The first of these two murders happened in the west of the county, literally on the banks of the Crinan Canal, built in the closing years of the 1700s, and inspired by projects down south and abroad, and by the necessities of speedy 'modern' travel and efficient industry. Stretching from Ardrishaig on the west shore of Loch Gilp, between the Knapdale hills and through the great Moine Mhor peat bog, to the inlets of the coast at Crinan, the canal was always a doubtful venture, needing constant repair and rebuilding, restablising of banks and supply reservoirs, and with doubtful finances behind it. In building the canal, the venture both created settlements and left already established ones high and dry on the banks, separated from their neighbours in Glassary parish.[2]

The little farmstead of Daill was one of these places left perched on the brink of the new canal, and in the autumn of 1804, one of the families living there was the MacArthurs, the father Neil, a shoemaker, his wife and their adult son, Duncan and his wife Betty, a Kintyre woman. The latter pair (Betty at least was in her early 30s, so Duncan was probably a similar age) had married just three years before, but due to being unable to find their own cottage, had stayed at the MacArthur's, while Duncan went out labouring. There'd as yet been no children of the marriage, and the two couples had lived relatively harmoniously in the shoemaker's tiny cottage.[3]

That autumn, Duncan moved temporarily to a neighbouring farm to help with the harvest, and Betty went down to Fernoch, just beyond Lochgilphead, for similar work. It seems however that Duncan had suspected there was something more than a professional relationship happening at Fernoch, so when Betty was due to walk to town one day in October to pay a debt, Duncan came home from Craiglass in order to accompany her. There must have been some tension in the cottage between Duncan and Betty that afternoon, since when he gave her a twenty shilling note to pay the debt with, stating that he'd accompany her to town, she refused. He demanded she give him the money back, and she refused that aswell. Further arguments from Duncan only made Betty dig her heels in more, even refusing to put on a proper pair of shoes or an extra petticoat, when he insisted. To modern eyes, (and perhaps even Duncan's parents, since old Neil asked his son to let Betty "make her own way" to town) his wife was dressed perfectly decently, but to Duncan (who may have been the controlling, coercive sort) she was inadequately dressed for the journey: a substantial petticoat worn as a skirt but with no extra petticoat below (only a shift), a short bodice-jacket, neckerchief, footless stockings, an indoor cap and her mother-in-law's long, thick cloak.[4]

Eventually, according to Duncan MacArthur, he allowed his wife to leave the cottage with the money, she stating that she wouldn't be returning the same day, (wise, considering it would be dark by the time she got to town), but would spend the night with a friend. He advised her to come back first thing in the morning however, as he'd hoped to go to church at Kilmichael with her, and she said she would. Duncan himself didn't "stir" from Daill all night, going to bed early because he was tired from working hard at the harvest, leaving his parents to put the light out, and go to bed themselves.[5]

Betty didn't arrive at her friend's in Lochgilphead. Neither did she arrive at Duncan Fisher's to pay the twenty shilling debt. She didn't arrive back at Daill first thing either, to go to church with her husband, although no-one seems to have picked up on the fact that it was a Thursday[6] (not a Sunday, as Duncan claimed in his first statement), and there's unlikely to have been a service on at the kirk. One person did arrive at Daill however that October morning: Jean Ross came knocking at the cottage door, saying a woman's body had been found in the canal, just by the swing bridge at Cairnbaan.[7]

Old Neil had only one exclamation to make: "Christ preserve us!". An exclamation made, perhaps, in shock, but with a hidden meaning when considered in retrospect. Shock or no, he, his son and another MacArthur man from Daill, made their way down to Cairnbaan to help with the retrieval of the body, and found some men there putting together a make-shift stretcher and lifting the poor woman's remains onto it – face down, as she was rather scantily dressed, and they wanted to preserve her modesty. At some stage it appears that the woman was turned over and one can imagine the shock Neil MacArthur, if not his son, got when he saw her face. It was his daughter-in-law, Betty, stripped of cloak and skirt, and with bruises and blood marks on her face, breast and neck, swollen arms and a ruddy face. She'd been lying on her back on the canal-bank, 50 or 60 yards downstream from the bridge, and with her feet in the water, and the grass around her much trodden.[8]

The men conveying the stretcher took poor Betty's remains to Cairnbaan; some of them suggested taking her further on to the kirk, for safety and decency, but the MacArthurs insisted she be brought back home to Daill, where she still was the following day when the local magistrates arrived. Despite Duncan's protestations, they had Betty's body removed to Kilmichael kirk, where she lay until Sunday. During that time, two local doctors were called in to perform a post mortem exam (one of them was Ensign MacArthur, who would be involved in the defence of the excise at the illegal still-house a couple of years later[9]), and the evidence from this was definite: Betty MacArthur had been strangled, certainly not drowned. Someone had clearly grabbed her left arm violently, knocked her onto her back on the grass of the canal-bank, knelt on her front (breaking a rib in the process, a classic injury for victims of strangling[10]), and throttled her, perhaps with her own neckerchief, as there isn't any mention of finger-marks on her neck. The poor woman may have put up quite a struggle, as there were scratches on her neck and arm, perhaps where she'd tried to fight off her attacker. Whoever had murdered her had then made off with her cloak and petticoat, and pushed her further down the bank, maybe hoping she would fall into the water and drown, if she wasn't already dead, or at least hiding her body for a few weeks until the force of nature brought her back to the surface.[11]

Meanwhile back at Daill, Duncan MacArthur, Betty's widower, was the chief suspect. The argument he'd had with his wife the previous night was paramount, and when the magistrates returned to the shoemaker's cottage in search of further evidence, they found something incriminating. In a chest there was a long, thick cloak identical to the one Betty had worn when she went out to Lochgilphead that evening. There seems to have been some confusion over this garment, as Duncan claimed that there were two of them, one given by his sister to Betty, before the former left the country with her new husband, and the other his mother's. There was a similar confusion over an identical petticoat, but the curious thing was that the cloak was soaking wet. Duncan didn't know how it had got so wet, and it's at this stage that he starts incriminating himself in his statements. He changes some details, adds too much irrelevant detail, and makes one significant claim that may have influenced the jury at his trial. No, he hadn't accompanied his wife along the canal-bank to Lochgilphead that fateful evening, but half a mile after she set out (supposedly alone), darkness fell.[12] How did he know that, if he hadn't been with her? Duncan had said he'd been very tired when he went to bed early that night, but one can't help wondering if it wasn't exhaustion from the harvest, but exhaustion from a walk down to Cairnbaan, a violent struggle with his wife, then a walk back again, along a bankside which would be almost pitch black, with only the silver ribbon of the canal, and his local knowledge, to guide him. Could the darkness have been the reason Betty didn't go fully into the water? Had he pushed her over the bank, intending her body to disappear, but the blackness of the night, with what little moonlight there was, prevented Duncan from seeing exactly how far he'd pushed her, and with perhaps a fear of being discovered, he left the scene.

With Duncan MacArthur in custody at Inveraray, and Betty's body presumably buried at Kilmichael during his absence behind bars, the wheels of criminal justice turned very ponderously at Inveraray. The case was certainly about to be tried at the circuit court, but they may have just missed the autumn hearings, as it took until spring for Duncan's case to be tried. One of the causes of the delay may have been the difficulty they had in tracing a key witness, Jean Ross and her husband Hugh, who perhaps were the first people who found Betty. Jean and Hugh had moved up to Corpach after the murder, and the authorities clearly had difficulty tracking them down, and even when they did it seems as though they weren't very keen on attending court; they were eventually persuaded, with the threat of a fine if they didn't. Another hitch in proceedings was a trial due to be heard of a man from Ardconnel near Oban, accused of a local assault and robbery, but this was adjourned (he may have been in jail with Duncan MacArthur), so that it could be dealt with by the Sheriff Court, where he was subsequently found not guilty.[13] The people at Inveraray clearly had a far more important trial to handle than a bit of local thieving and fighting.

In court that spring, and infront of Advocate Charlie Hope, Duncan's own parents were questioned as to their son's behaviour on the fateful night. His father's testimony only really enlarges on the scene when Betty's body was found, but his mother (her feelings must have been acutely mixed; giving testimony which could see her son hanged, but clearly trying to tell the truth) described some telling moments. Both her son and Betty went out together that evening to walk to Lochgilphead and when he returned alone and she asked what had become of her daughter-in-law, Duncan said she wouldn't allow him to accompany her. They'd not all gone to bed, but had waited up for Betty, as she'd said she would return that night. When Duncan's mother was questioned about how long Duncan had been away from the cottage 'accompanying' Betty along the canal-bank, one can almost hear her confusion and distress, since, after being so specific with the other details, she says she can't tell how long her son was away.[14]

Whoever it was that gave the crucial testimony in court, the jury (a classic Inveraray mix of gentry, farmers, artisans, merchants, lawyers, and even a changehouse keeper from Rothesay), the verdict came back a resounding proven, and therefore guilty of murder at Cairnbaan. The claim from a clerk of court that the crime happened further down the canal at Craiglass can be taken with a pinch of salt, as it came from a man who later confused some important details about another murder,[15] and was far from local, compared to the evidence given by several local witnesses who found Betty's body by the swing bridge.[16]

There are two twists to the end of the story about the Cairnbaan wife murderer. The first came in court from the mouth of Advocate Charlie Hope – naturally, Duncan MacArthur was to be hanged, but instead of this happening at Inveraray, as all except three hangings in nearly 140 years had been,[17] it was to happen at the murder site by the Crinan Canal. Possibly, Baronet Hope had in mind the effect on the traffic which passed through the canal such an occasion would have; perhaps he even wanted to acknowledge the rising economic importance of Lochgilphead, and was thinking about the impact of Inveraray justice on an increasing population. More likely however was a ruling by the Lords of Justiciary in Edinburgh a few years before, that a criminal sentenced to hang should serve such a sentence at the crime-site.[18] There were several heated discussions over the ruling in future years, but clearly Baronet Hope interpreted the ruling to the letter. Whatever the reason, a hanging anywhere must have come as a bit of a shock to the Inveraray magistrates. Quite simply, they didn't have a hangman, let alone, probably a gallows.[19]

The last hanging at Inveraray before Duncan MacArthur had been the two women thieves who'd done some nefarious work at the Glassary market, but that had been in 1753,[20] and since then there's evidence that the burgh didn't have a hangman until the time of Willie Stewart in 1792.[21] He however had apparently retired within ten years, leaving the post open. Whatever had happened to the old Inveraray gallows is not evident either, but the last one would have been of the old traditional style (two uprights, a beam across at the top, and a couple of ladders), and certain 'improvements' had been made recently to this design, incorporating a stage, a trap door, and steps.[22]

The nearest place which had both a hangman and a gallows was Glasgow, and it wasn't an unknown scenario for a smaller burgh to borrow a larger one's staff and equipment at the time of an execution, any gallows essentially being collapsible for storage and transport. So it was that the Glasgow hangman, one Archie MacArthur (the irony of the surname must have been commented on!), a stout young man and former soldier who'd only been in the job a year, arrived (probably by boat) at Inveraray with his 'modern' design of gallows. The whole party, hangman, gallows, assistant, minister, jailer and the accused may well have travelled to Crinan along the canal, coming in at Ardrishaig and probably trailing locals in its wake along the towpath as it travelled.[23]

The current site of the gallows is now a boat yard, looking out over the canal to the Cairnbaan Hotel. It's here that the second twist in the tragedy comes in the form of a nearby Neolithic cairn, hence 'Cairnbaan'. The exact location of this cairn is now almost untraceable, being swamped with boggy vegetation, but in the 1970s it had an inscribed design on one of its keystones, the significance of which may have been lost on the archaeologists who copied it down. The inscription bears a strong resemblance to an old-fashioned gibbet. With the presence of Archie MacArthur's 'modern' gallows at the hanging site, the inscription probably doesn't depict the actual device used to send the shoemaker's son to meet his maker, but did one of the watching crowd on the canal-bank that day in 1804, perhaps waiting for the arrival of the boat carrying the dreaded party, scratch the depiction on the cairn, anticipating that a more old-fashioned device would be used?[24]

Inveraray hangings at this time were normally between 2 and 4pm[25], so the party may have made it back to town just in time for dusk. One can imagine the solemn procession, complete with the parish coffin, which wound its way from the lamp-lit pier to Surgeon Anderson's house, where the body was to be dissected. Any Inveraray folk watching probably assumed they'd never witness such a procession again. How wrong could they be?

Just over three years after Duncan MacArthur had been hanged at Cairnbaan, another wife murderer was sentenced to the same fate in Argyll, and again the murder involved water.

Over in Perthshire, a family by the name of MacDougall were sub-tenanting a croft at Balinbeg. They were better known locally as MacLaggan, and comprised the father John, who also earnt an extra living travelling to Argyll and back regularly to collect rags, which he bought from customers with new crockery. His wife had died, and he'd remarried, having already had a family including at least one son, Peter. By the beginning of winter 1806, Peter was twenty years old and had got married himself to a local woman, Mary Stewart, the daughter of a kirk beadle. The family were hardly well-off, but they worked hard, Peter doing farm labouring (although he'd trained as a shoemaker), Mary making-do with her clothes, and Peter and his father farming their wee patch of land in summer; they weren't technically tinkers, as has been claimed, and stayed under cover when on their travels to Argyll, though they may have had tinker heritage if they possessed a pony and cart, and tinkers from that district were known to frequent the Argyll roads.[26]

Peter seems to have been a simple sort, and may not have been in the strongest of health, but he and Mary set off ahead of his father and stepmother one Friday early in December, around midday. They stayed that night near Aberfeldy, before continuing on their way through Breadalbane and Strath Fillan and into Argyll. Peter's father and stepmother met the couple near Tyndrum, with the pony and cart, and they carried on, probably visiting regular customers, and exchanging some crockery for the rags.[27] Such redundant textiles would eventually be sold at a market, probably the one back at Moulin kirk in spring[28], or perhaps remade or cannabalised for buttons or lace before being sold on.

There was a small but flourishing market for such rags at the time (especially at Moulin), although it wasn't until later decades and the influx of Irish immigrants that it really took off in the cities.[29]

By the time the MacLaggans arrived at the changehouse of Inveroran on the night of Wednesday 10th December, the place may have been too full to accommodate them, so they spent the night nearby at Druimliart.[30] The MacLaggans may well have met the Fletchers who tenanted the changehouse [31], amongst other locals and travellers who were there that night, perhaps including Archie MacIntyre, a cottager from way over at the head of Loch Etive[32]. The MacLaggans had been covering around ten or eleven miles a day with their cart of crockery and rags, but the winter weather was probably coming in rather blowy and wet by then, so when, the following evening, they came through the Blackmount and saw ahead in the gloaming, the blessed sight of the King's House inn at the mouth of Glencoe, set amid the forbidding rocky slopes and under the lowering skies, it must have come as a relief. Even better, the place had enough room for them to stay. With the pony and its load (even if not the cart) presumably stashed somewhere under cover, the MacLaggans settled down for the evening until bedtime.[33]

At one point that evening, Peter MacLaggan and his wife may have had some sort of argument. Certainly, when he told Mary to go upstairs and get their bed ready (the place had been built as a changehouse, with a large upstairs room filled with beds which the guests had to set up for themselves) she took umbrage to it, and argued all the more. Eventually, thoroughly cheesed off, she demanded the changehouse keeper's wife unbolt the main door for her, and she stormed off into the night. Peter immediately followed, and the door was secured behind the couple.[34]

King's House still sits at the brink of the River Etive, a 'mean beast' of a water course even at its mildest, although the length passing King's House is quiet enough for modern kayakers to practise their beginner's lessons there, if the river isn't in spate.[35] The current bridge over the river may be the original, built when the military road was first laid down in the 1750s.[36] Both road and bridge however were repaired frequently, and King's House was, and still is, a popular stop-off for travellers. Unfortunately, it also sits dangerously close (or at least dangerous in the old days, without benefit of modern outdoor lighting) to the river, and in the filthy dark night such as prevailed outside the changehouse that Thursday evening, it would be easy for a stranger to the district to step too far off the path.

Whether this is what happened to Mary MacLaggan, or whether she and Peter continued their argument outdoors and he pushed her, we'll never know. He later implied that when he went outside, a mere few seconds later, she wasn't there. Mere seconds is all it would take for Mary, tired, disorientated and unable to see in the darkness the difference between river bank and road, to step off the track and fall into the river. The true situation may have been somewhere between the two scenarios, but whatever happened, Peter said that he stayed outdoors for an hour looking for his wife, with some other guests joining him; he would have stayed longer but the changehouse keeper encouraged him to wait until morning, since the weather was so bad.[37]

Fairly early on that Friday morning, old John MacLaggan set out from King's House, leaving Peter to continue searching for Mary. With no sign of her, Peter went along the road further towards Glencoe (to Altnafeich), then with still no sign of her, returned to King's House, and went in the opposite direction, saying later that he hoped Mary had set off on the road for home. When he couldn't find her as far as Bridge of Orchy, he came back to King's House again after dusk, presumably having taken a lift on someone's cart, in order to cover such distances in that time. No-one had seen Mary since the family passed that way the day before and his father, stepmother, cart, pony, and the load had also gone onto Glencoe.[38]

Meanwhile, Mary MacLaggan's body had been moving down the River Etive the previous night, in spate as it was, and viciously swelling and tearing her clothes such as only watercourses like the Etive can do.[39] Come the morning, with the countryside battered, and dishevelled, the flooded waters of the Etive would already be pulling away from the fields and river banks, depositing branches and chunks of turf in its wake. Did the receding waters of the river also deposit some tragic remains?

At a certain point in Glen Etive, the river passes through the gorge of Eas an Fhith Mor, (now beloved of advanced kayakers, and known locally as the worst spot on the river for rapids and waterfalls[40]) and it's been suggested by an experienced local waterman that this could be one of the places where a body could be held against the rocks, probably visible from horseback on the road at top or bottom of the rocky pass.[41]

Between the time of Peter's father and stepmother leaving King's House on the Friday morning and Peter meeting up with them again in Glencoe on the Saturday, it's not recorded where the older couple went. But one can judge how far they travelled by the distances the family covered on their way from Perthshire to Argyll, ie. ten or eleven miles a day.[42] With the middle of Glencoe (where he met Peter over 24 hours later) being only five miles from King's House, where had the couple gone during those intervening hours? The only place the MacLaggans could go to, is down the side road into Glen Etive, where the river carrying the remains of their daughter-in-law would be grumbling away beside the road. If the MacLaggans travelled through Glen Etive in the 'missing' twelve hours, in order to make it back to habitation to stay the night, then onto Glencoe to meet Peter, they would need to have turned back approximately 3½ miles into the glen – yet there doesn't seem to have been a settlement there at the time to give them cause to stop and perhaps do some selling of crockery and pick up some rags. So why would John MacLaggan appear to go down that side road into Glen Etive, only to turn round in an area apparently of no habitation?

Coincidentally, in this same vicinity is the Eas an Fhith Mor gorge where the body of Mary MacLaggan may have been held by the rocks and the receding waters.

Did Peter's father and stepmother find Mary's body, partly stripped by the fierce currents, and, panicking and anxious to distance themselves from the tragic scene, they freed her from the rocks, pitched her back into the river, then returned to Glencoe? John certainly seemed to know something more than is being stated in the court records, and those missing twelve hours wouldn't appear to be explicable in any other way.[43]

Where Peter's father and stepmother spent the Friday night whilst Peter was back at King's House again isn't explained in the old records, but they may have stayed at Altnafeich, before travelling on the following morning partly into Glencoe, where they eventually met up with Peter.[44]

By that time, Mary's body would have moved onto the head of Loch Etive, where the tragic remains were discovered the next day. It may have been Archie MacIntyre, the tenant at Gualachulain, who saw an anomaly on the sandbanks and bogs at the river mouth early on the Saturday morning and went to investigate. He was certainly among the witnesses at the later trial.[45]

The normal circumstances surrounding the discovery of an unidentified body at that time are hinted at with the case of the Crinan Canal murderer – Mary's remains may have been taken to a kirk, or any good sized building with some reasonable security and a spare room or two. A local JP or magistrate was probably notified, perhaps by word of mouth from a reliable local figure, although in Mary MacLaggan's case, with the enormous size of the parish, it may have taken a few days for the information to reach Inveraray. At some stage however, someone appears to have identified poor Mary's half-clothed body, perhaps the Fletchers at Inveroran, who'd met her on the journey from Perthshire to King's House.

Meanwhile, the MacLaggans had gone onto Appin, then probably through Benderloch and onto Taynuilt via one of the ferries over the loch (the Connel ferry could take a pony and cart[46]). The family were heading for Inveraray to get some more crockery to pay their customers with, so probably stayed at the Taynuilt changehouse on the way. From there, they'd have travelled onward to Inveraray, bought their crockery from one of the several general stores in the town, and thus loaded down and ready for business again, set off to Lochgilphead by boat, then northwards to Oban, gathering rags and swapping them for crockery along the way.

The family came into Oban on a Saturday night. The village was occupied at the time by the 2nd battalion of the

91st Regiment, with their recruiting officers, though such recruiting wouldn't be enacted on the Sunday morning. Come first thing on the Monday though, or perhaps on the Sunday afternoon, old John MacLaggan made a suggestion to his son Peter. The latter was now without a wife (how did either man know that for sure?) and Sgt Robertson was looking for volunteers. Peter's father told him to offer a different name to the recruiting officer, and so father and son parted for what, as far as the older man knew, would be the last time they met. Certainly, it would be the last time they parted with Peter as a free man.[47]

The regiment was leaving the town that same day, and Peter, known by his commanding officer as Duncan Robertson and looking forward to the 11 guineas promised to every volunteer at that time,[48] left with it, heading for Taynuilt, where they'd have stayed the night. The following day, they marched to Dalmally, and stopped at the changehouse there, then onwards to Tyndrum – the very same place where the MacLaggan family had stopped on the other leg of their journey, and Peter had doubtless met the Fletchers there. It seems as though the news of Mary MacLaggan's death in the River Etive had gone the full rounds of the parish and neighbouring districts by then, and the Fletchers may well have been the ones to alert the regiment to the young Perthshire soldier in their ranks. Peter MacDougall, otherwise known as MacLaggan, now going by the name of Duncan Robertson, was arrested there and then, and while the regiment marched onwards, the sergeant turned back with Peter for Dalmally.

By this time, it was around Christmas[49], and however quietly Christmas was celebrated north of the border in the old days, it seems that someone took the opportunity to get a round of drinks in once the sergeant and his arrested soldier arrived back at Dalmally changehouse. With alcohol loosening his tongue, Peter started talking, and confessed to the argument with his wife that filthy dark night by the King's House inn. He also confessed to killing her, but whether this was the truth or the drink talking or he just felt himself guilty after perhaps pushing her in the course of the argument, we'll never know. With such an admission and with witnesses there (including a parish constable from Perthshire) there was only one place the sergeant could take Peter – over the hill on the military road to Inveraray, where they arrived almost a week after Peter had enlisted.[50]

With Christmas, New Year and some bad winter weather restricting the court proceedings, it took over a fortnight until Peter could be examined in front of an Advocate, and he made his first statement. From then on, the usual court processes occurred, with Mary's body being subject to a post mortem, the clerk of court receiving her clothes as evidence, witnesses and jurors being called and statements taken from all and sundry. Unfortunately for modern historians, the crucial statements of these witnesses appear to have been lost, and we may never know who exactly it was who recognised Peter at Tyndrum, who retrieved Mary's body, and who, if anyone, went out into the dark night to help look for her, after she'd stormed off. It is however at this stage that someone makes a huge mistake about the date of the murder, quoting the 15th of December (a Monday, not a Thursday) and under the impression that King's House was a good eight miles further south than it is/was. It was spring by this time, and the trial was set for the end of April.

The circuit court judge, Lord Meadowbank hadn't been best pleased when he arrived at Dalmally on the journey from Glasgow to find that there was no carriage waiting for him to transport him to town, only a card apologising and a horse and presumably a groom or a court assistant to guide him over the hill.[51] In front of a disgruntled Lord Meadowbank the clerk who'd made the mistake about the date and location was probably in for a good roasting, and certainly the case had to be adjourned for a full five months as a result of it. Eventually, with the advice of Lord Meadowbank regarding the prisoner's health not being acted upon, the prisoner himself asking for a swift trial and not to have "much confinement",[52] and the glitch in the criminal charge sorted out, the case re-opened a full ten months after Mary MacLaggan's death.

What small hints we can pick up of the personality of the various figures associated with the trial only serve to enlighten the scene in the court room at Inveraray. Sgt Robertson, with typical military flair gives his full title and regimental designation (one wonders if he stood to attention in court, and barked out his name, rank and number!); Advocate Henry Erskine, probably having heard from his colleague Meadowbank about the behaviour of the bungling clerk, may have sat there, annoyed at the whole proceedings; the (very!) young minister MacGibbon, barely into the parish[53], who translated Peter's Perthshire Gaelic; and the wealthy, middle-aged surgeon (with his loyalty to Inveraray, its people and court[54]) John Anderson who'd done the postmortem on Mary MacLaggan.

All these people bring colour to a proceedings which ultimately ended in a solemn declaration by the jury: guilty of murder. Peter MacLaggan was sent back to the tolbooth cell to be fed only on bread and water until the enactment of his sentence, some 7½ weeks ahead.[55]

Yet again, the Inveraray magistrates had to find a hangman and some gallows, but this time Henry Erskine seemed to prefer interpreting the former decision of the Lords Justiciary in a more practical way. The hanging, instead of being way out at King's House on a wet winter's day, with all the expense and transport difficulties that would entail, ordered that it should be out at Craig na Caorach, close to the Cromalt burn and on the edge of the burgh boundary.[56] It was to here that Archie MacArthur and his equipment travelled one afternoon in mid November 1807, the exact spot now lost, perhaps under modern road building, a boat yard or the undergrowth and rockfalls by the loch.[57] Within an hour of leaving the tolbooth, Peter MacLaggan would be dead, the last known hanging at Inveraray, and the end of an era. There were others, criminals who would normally be sentenced to death, (although some were declared insane or found Not Proven)[58], but transferrals to an Edinburgh jail[59], commutations to transportation[60], a Royal Pardon[61], or the criminal going outlaw in the first place[62], ensured that there would be no more dire processions to the town limits, no more borrowing of the hangman and no more dissections under John Anderson's roof followed by a clandestine burial of what remained of the body. Quite where Peter (and Duncan MacArthur before him) were buried after their dissection isn't recorded. What remained of the bodies of dissected criminals were often dumped unceremoniously somewhere nearby, often in a mass grave or any handy piece of unconsecrated ground, occasionally even on the town midden or in the surgeon's garden[63], but John Anderson does seem to have had a more compassionate disposition, and it's to be hoped he had the remains interred in an unmarked corner of Kilmalieu.[64]

The roads which the MacLaggans travelled on throughout their Argyll journeyings those winter days in 1806 are and were a reflection of how time had changed in Argyll. Indeed Inveraray itself had finally made the move to a new site, with the old one wiped out above ground, and the new military road which the regiment had been building when one of them killed the old soldier back in 1759, now finished, walls and roadsides, pier and bridges now built, rebuilt and stabilised. The change of site for the town also matched a gradual change of opinion over time on law-breakers and prison conditions, and the start of a campaign for prison reform[65], which would lead, later in the century, to questions on the validity of capital punishment. A new wave of feeling on crime and criminals was emerging, and in some ways Inveraray was ahead of its time. The cities and some other towns continued hanging convicted murderers well into the 19th and 20th centuries, but it does appear that Peter MacLaggan was the last at Inveraray. This doesn't necessarily mean that the Inveraray courts were more compassionate, and it may be that sheer expense at the upkeep of a hangman who didn't get much work prevented them from sending anyone else to Craig na Caorach. Whatever the cause, from the vast wind-battered moors of the Blackmount to the parchment coloured sands of Kintyre, Argyll, its law abiding people and its criminals, had seen the last of the bodies swinging on a gallows rope by Loch Fyne. A new era was dawning.

FOOTNOTES

1. As can be imagined, a multiplicity of sources including "The Argyll Justiciary Records volume 1, 1664-1705" published by the Stair society, 1949, pp.3,33-34,43,76,111,142,158,167,177,179; Ibid. volume 2, published 1969, pp.230,239,365,379,383,515; "Accused and Persewed, murder, riot and theft in old Argyll", by Lindsay Campbell, published Matador, Leicestershire 2019, pp.46,64-70; "Ane Compact of Villany, the history of Argyll's outlawed gang" by Lindsay Campbell, published Matador, Leicestershire, 2015, pp.26-27, 78, 87-88; "Highland Papers vol 3", by JRN MacPhail, published Scottish History Society, 2nd series, volume XX, published 1920, pp.37; "Now Prisoner Within, murder, riot and crime in old Argyll", by Lindsay Campbell, published Matador, Leicestershire, 2017, pp. 22-23; Certan Crymes booklet number 1 "Cover the Corps, the Cologin murder", by Lindsay Campbell, privately printed 2018.
2. Numerous pages within "The Crinan Canal" by Marian Pallister, published Birlinn, Edinburgh 2016.
3. JC13/33/44v; JC26/1804/37 and 39, at the National Records of Scotland, Edinburgh.
4. Ibid.
5. Ibid.
6. timeanddate.com
7. JC13/33/44v; JC26/1804/37 and 39 in the National Records of Scotland, Edinburgh.
8. Ibid.
9. JC13/34f; JC26/1805/15 in the National Records of Scotland, Edinburgh.
10. "Murder Houses of London" by Jan Bondeson, published Amberly, Gloucestershire, 2015, p.203.
11. JC13/33/44v; JC26/1804/37 and 39 in the National Records of Scotland, Edinburgh.
12. JC26/1804/39 in the National Records of Scotland, Edinburgh.
13. JC13/33/44v; JC26/1804/37 and 39 in the National Records of Scotland, Edinburgh.
14. Ibid.
15. JC26/1807/20; JC26/1807/47; JC13/35/8, in the National Records of Scotland, Edinburgh.
16. JC13/33/44v; JC26/1804/37 and 39 in the National Records of Scotland, Edinburgh.
17. References to criminals who were tried at Inveraray, but hanged

outwith the burgh include "The Argyll Justiciary Records volume 1, 1664-1705" published by the Stair society, 1949, pp.10 and 35; "The Encyclopaedia of Scottish Executions, 1750-1963" by Alex F.Young, published Eric Dobby Publishing Ltd, Kent, 1998, p.43.
18. "The Encyclopaedia of Scottish Executions, 1750-1963" by Alex F.Young, published Eric Dobby Publishing Ltd, Kent, 1998, p.68.
19. Inveraray Burgh Minutes (document B1/1/1-2) at Argyll and Bute County archives ("Live Argyll"), Manse Brae, Lochgilphead, where the hangman's salary was accounted as part of the burgh income in 1755.
20. "The Encyclopaedia of Scottish Executions, 1750-1963" by Alex F.Young, published Eric Dobby Publishing Ltd, Kent, 1998, p.45.
21. Inveraray Burgh Minutes (document B1/1/1-2) at Argyll and Bute County archives ("Live Argyll"), Manse Brae, Lochgilphead.
22. "The Encyclopaedia of Scottish Executions, 1750-1963" by Alex F.Young, published Eric Dobby Publishing Ltd, Kent, 1998, p.2-3.
23. Ibid. pp.69, 152-3, 158.
24. Royal Commission for Ancient Historical Monuments in Scotland, Inventory no.6, Mid Argyll and Cowal, prehistory and early history including monuments, published 1988, p.57. See also "The Encyclopaedia of Scottish Executions, 1750-1963" by Alex F.Young, published Eric Dobby Publishing Ltd, Kent, 1998, p.1, illustration of the "Weird Gibbet Stone".
25. "The Argyll Justiciary Records volume 1, 1664-1705" published by the Stair society, 1949, pp.505,515,517.
26. JC26/1807/20 in the National Records of Scotland, Edinburgh.; testimony of Kay Liney, Moulin Heritage Centre, to whom the author is indebted.
27. Ibid.
28. Pitlochry and Moulin heritage centre fact sheet no.2, available online.
29. The famous Paddy's Market in Glasgow (a veritable hub for the west coast rag trade in former times) reputedly has its origins with the settlement of Irish emigrants in the vicinity of Shipbank Lane, off the Briggait, but probably not until the 1820s at the earliest. Before then, the district was rather more high-class, cf.archive. org/stream/Paddy'smarket; "The Heart of Glasgow" by Jack House, published Richard Drew Publishing, Glasgow, 1982, pp.79-80.
30. JC26/1807/20 in the National Records of Scotland, Edinburgh.
31. JC13/35/40-44, witness list; JC26/1807/20 in the National Records of Scotland, Edinburgh.
32. Ibid.

33. JC26/1807/20 in the National Records of Scotland,Edinburgh. For a contemporary description of King's House, see "Recollections of a Tour in Scotland" by Dorothy Wordsworth, published Forgotten Books, 2012, p.176-7, pp.176-7.
34. JC26/1807/20 in the National Records of Scotland,Edinburgh.
35. Testimony of Laura Bennit and Mark Mitchell, Sea Kayak, Oban, to whom the author is indebted; www.eatsleepkayak.com; www.ukriversguidebook.co.uk
36. The National Library of Scotland, map room website (maps.nls.uk/Scotland/index.html) for General Roy's map and George Langlands map.
37. JC26/1807/20, in the National Records of Scotland,Edinburgh.
38. Ibid.
39. Testimony of Laura Bennit and Mark Mitchell, Sea Kayak, Oban.
40. www.eatsleepkayak.com; www.ukriversguidebook.co.uk
41. Testimony of Ewan MacLellan, water bailiff, to whom the author is indebted for his unsurpassable local knowledge, and opinion as to where on the River Etive a dead body could be trapped. One of these places could be at the Eas an Fhith More gorge, but the small body of water known as Lochan Urr may also have been the location, as it readily floods from the river, when the latter is in spate. However, this lochan doesn't appear to have existed before the time of the first Ordnance Survey maps, and may have only been cut out as a small reservoir or pleasure lochan in early Victorian times.
42. JC26/1807/20 in the National Records of Scotland,Edinburgh.
43. The author's site visit to the glen summer 2019, and the many hours of calculation at home, using the Ordnance Survey Pathfinder maps, the average time the MacLaggans spent on the road, personal knowledge of dawn and dusk times in Argyll in December, and observations on several local watercourses to calculate the speed of the River Etive in spate, at mph, in order to compare the travels of Peter and his father and stepmother, between Inveroran/Bridge of Orchy and Glencoe. To lay out in detail the results of this work would be too lengthy for this footnote, however the conclusion reached was that any other timing and routes travelled by Peter and his father would mean that either they missed each other completely while on the road or met up at King's House instead of Glencoe.
44. JC26/1807/20 in the National Records of Scotland,Edinburgh.
45. JC13/35/40-44, list of witnesses, in the National Records of Scotland, Edinburgh.

46. "Recollections of a Tour in Scotland, 1803" by Dorothy Wordsworth, published Forgotten Books, 2012, p.153-4.
47. JC26/1807/20 in the National Records of Scotland, Edinburgh; timeanddate.com
48. "Collins Encyclopaedia of Scotland" edited by John Keay and Julia Keay, published Harper Collins, London, 1994, p.697.
49. timeanddate.com
50. JC26/1807/20, in the National Records of Scotland, Edinburgh.
51. JC13/35/8 in the National Records of Scotland, Edinburgh.
52. There has been much confusion over the issue of the date of the murder, but it certainly appears that the mix-up was caused by the bungling clerk getting the days of the week wrong (cf. JC26/1807/20; JC26/1807/47; JC13/35/8 in the National Records of Scotland, Edinburgh). The author has spent much time attempting to untangle this mix-up of the dates and days, and the timescale presented here would appear to be the most logical.
53. JC13/35/40-44; "Fasti Ecclesiae Scoticanae, the succession of ministers in the Church of Scotland from the Reformation" volume 4, Synods of Argyll, Perth and Stirling, by Hew Scott, published Forgotten Books, London, 2017, p.10.
54. In Dr. Anderson's will, he had several debtors from amongst the people of Inveraray, and several sources detail his work for the courts and the town for decades (scotlandspeople website, wills, 1842; see also note 64 below).
55. JC13/35/40-44 in the National Records of Scotland, Edinburgh.
56. Ibid. Much has been made of an account taken in the 1880s from one Anne Campbell in Inveraray who as a little girl witnessed the last hanging in the town. Her account however has so many inaccuracies (the hangman, the postholes for the gallows, the burial site, the age and health of the accused, even the year date) that in old age she may have confused at least one later Glasgow hanging with her own misperception at the time and possibly what she was later told by her parents. Even the location of the hanging could thus be cast in doubt, as the court papers only specify "a common place for executions" and there hadn't been any for over fifty years. The author will leave the solution to these enigmas to Inveraray historians, but is happy to provide copies of her research notes. Ref: "Records of Argyll" by Lord Archibald Campbell, published Blackwood & sons, Edin 1885, p.54.
57. Testimony of Ken MacTaggart, Inveraray and the Inveraray Historical Society, to all of whom the author is indebted.

58. Several cases eg. JC13/36 (Margaret MacPhadain, Ballahaugh, 1809 or Alex MacLean, Morvern, 1805) in the National Records of Scotland, Edinburgh.
59. Several cases eg.JC8/10 (Nathaniel Blair, 1814) in the National Records of Scotland,Edinburgh.
60. Several cases eg.JC13/33 (John Ferguson, Whitehouses) in the National Records of Scotland,Edinburgh.
61. Several cases eg. JC13/38/3; JC4/5 pp.443b-445a; JC27/117 or JC13/37 (Constantine O'Neal, Bute 1809) in the National Records of Scotland,Edinburgh.
62. Several cases eg. JC8/10 (Donald Campbell, Glenorchy parish, 1814) in the National Records of Scotland,Edinburgh.
63. Several sources online, the general consensus being whether the dissection was legal and whether the surgeon or teaching institution had a garden, or if there was a town midden nearby. The remains of legal dissections appear to have been deposited in paupers' mass graves, or unconsecrated corners of a burial ground, cf.www.thesun.co.uk, 5.11.19; "The Story of Crime and Punishment", BBC History Magazine collector's edition, published Immediate Medium Company, Bristol, 2018, pp.62 and 65.
64. Dr.John Anderson appears to have been one of the supporters of the movement for prison reform, or at least a new prison in Inveraray, as he petitions the court for the early release of a prisoner, stating that the latter's health would be affected if he stayed behind bars much longer ("Warrants of Commitment and Liberation", B32/2/3, Argyll & Bute County Archives ("Live Argyll"), Manse Brae, Lochgilphead). Anderson also passed the new prison as being "quite dry and free from damp" when it was built ("The Acts of Sederunt of the Lords and Council of Session, 1796-1800", published Bell and Bradfute, 1800, via Google Books, p.13). The land outside the north wall of Kilmalieu is considerably higher than that within the wall. This may be due to the land originally there being higher, successive grass-cutters depositing their load (it's currently accessible due to the crumbling walls), or it may indicate a history of unconsecrated burials, classically undertaken on the north side of any church grounds, the site of the original Kilmalieu church not being far from this spot.
65. "The Story of Crime and Punishment", BBC History Magazine collector's edition, published Immediate Medium Company, Bristol, 2018, p.8,88-89; "The Encyclopaedia of Scottish Executions, 1750-1963" by Alex F.Young, published Eric Dobby Publishing Ltd, Kent, 1998, p.158; "A History of London

Life", by RJ Mitchell and MDR Leys, published Pelican Books Ltd, Middlesex, 1963, pp.233-4; "Encyclopaedia Britannica", macropaedia volume 14, pp.1098-9 and micropaedia volume 5, p.159.

OTHER WORKS BY LINDSAY CAMPBELL,
PUBLISHED BY MATADOR

Ane Compact of Villany, the history of Argyll's outlawed gang.

Now Prisoner Within, murder, riot and crime in old Argyll.

Accused and Persewed, murder, riot and theft in old Argyll.

THE CERTAN CRYMES
SERIES OF BOOKLETS,
PRIVATELY PUBLISHED

Cover the Corps, the Cologin murder.

Under Cloud of Night, the Knapdale smugglers.

Ane Bussh of Heather, the Minard murder.

A Damned Scoundrel, the Lochgilphead poisonings.

Matador

For exclusive discounts on Matador titles,
sign up to our occasional newsletter at
troubador.co.uk/bookshop